Contents

INTRODUCTION

English Works! is an interactive video and textbook program for high-beginning and intermediate ESL students in or about to enter the workplace. It provides instruction in the essential communication skills adult learners need to succeed on the job. The ten video segments along with the corresponding student text feature well-researched, authentic problems derived from actual workplace situations and incidents. The video episodes include five main characters who represent the cultural and ethnic diversity of the American workforce. The episodes take place in one of five typical workplace sites: a hotel, a hospital, a retirement home, a convenience store, and a maintenance site.

Video is a powerful medium for teaching listening skills and culture because it provides a contextualized opportunity for learners to make sense of auditory information. Nonetheless, it is important to recognize that listening in a new language is a challenging task because of the heavy constraints it puts on memory and on processing information. The **English Works!** video episodes have been made as accessible as possible to ESL students by providing a rich context in which the language can be understood. Conversations are presented in natural language and at a natural speaking speed. The video segments have intentionally been kept quite short to allow learners to develop some listening strategies. In fact, intermediate students can usually focus only for 30 seconds to a minute and a half because the demand on their memory and cognitive processing is so great. Wherever possible, settings, props, action, and interaction have been provided that parallel and elucidate the dialogue, allowing learners to use their prior knowledge to facilitate understanding.

Although listening constitutes a major part of everyone's daily communication (most people spend 60% of every day listening), few instructional materials provide instruction in *learning to listen.* An important principle of listening instruction is to acknowledge and enlist each learner's prior knowledge to facilitate understanding. Adult learners learn more effectively when instructional materials respect and build on their prior experiences. **English Works!** uses a strategy-based approach to learning to listen. Focusing on the listening process improves learners' ability to listen to authentic language. It also empowers learners to be more independent; they know how to listen and are able to continue listening in challenging situations outside of the classroom, especially on the job.

English Works! provides opportunities for students to practice their newly acquired language skills to improve communication in the workplace and in their own everyday world. The speaking instruction focuses attention on critical interaction patterns, including conversation management strategies. Learners role-play situations with their classmates and are also encouraged to reflect on and compare how, when, and where the interactions arise in their culture. Cultural information about the American workplace that can help students get and keep jobs is presented in each video segment.

English
WORKS!

Joan Rubin

Sharon McKay

Inaam Mansoor

Arlington Public Schools (Va.)

Longman

English Works!

Copyright © 1995 by Addison-Wesley Publishing Company, Inc.

Longman, 10 Bank Street, White Plains, NY 10606

Photo credits: Arlington Public Schools, Arlington, VA

Acquisitions editor: Anne Boynton-Trigg
Development editor: Debbie Sistino
Production editor: Liza Pleva
Text design: Circa 86, Inc.
Cover design: Edward Smith Design, Inc
Cover photos: Arlington Public Schools, Arlington, VA

Library of Congress Cataloging in Publication Data

Rubin, Joan. 1932-
    English works! / Joan Rubin, Sharon McKay, Inaam Mansoor.
        p. cm.
    ISBN 0-201-87681-7
    1. English language—Textbooks for foreign speakers. I. McKay.
    Sharon. II. Mansoor, Inaam. III. Title
PE1128.R75 1995
428.2'4—dc20   95-1983
                                                      CIP

1 2 3 4 5 6 7 8 9 10-CRS-98979695

English Works! features a strategy-based approach to reading workplace documents, specifically job announcements and work forms. The lesson on reading a job announcement teaches the strategy of finding the more important parts of the document in order to prepare for the application and interview process. The lesson on work forms provides strategies for reading some of the simpler forms workers may encounter.

ORGANIZATION OF THE LESSONS

Every video segment has an accompanying unit in the Student Book. Each section of the video is labeled to correspond to a section in the text so you can find each section easily. Each of units provides opportunities to learn how to use an array of learning strategies, first listening strategies followed by speaking and reading activities.

Learning to Listen	Speaking and Reading Activities
Thinking About the Topic	Check Your Understanding
First Impressions	Language Skills
Brainstorm	Conversation Practice
Confirm	Summary
Main Idea	Cultural Exchange
Predict	Contact Assignment
Action Plan	
Listening for Detail	

TEACHING LISTENING–"LEARNING TO LISTEN"

English Works! can help you teach listening strategically. The purpose of the *Learning to Listen* section is to provide students with a skill—how to listen. It focuses on the process, not on understanding each and every word, but rather on learning how to focus and to begin to construct the meaning. Listening involves making sense of information that comes from many sources: language, tone of voice, background knowledge, context, gestures, action, interaction, and prior text. The exercises in *Learning to Listen* focus on these different information sources. Drawing students' attention to the different components of a message provides them with tools to begin listening on their own.

The best way to teach listening is to go through *Learning to Listen* strategy by strategy. It is extremely helpful to announce to learners what you are focusing on. For example, "Now we are going to *Think about the Topic*." In addition, it can help to say, "When you think about a topic, it helps you prepare to listen." In this way, learners have a label and a reason for using this strategy. Once you have announced the strategy you can follow the instructions given in the text.

Thinking About the Topic

The first strategy gets learners to think about the topic of the lesson, and activates any vocabulary students already have. It also gives an indication of what students already know about the topic. Since the initial focus is on helping learners become more independent by using what they already know to help them listen, we strongly recommend that teachers do not provide any new vocabulary at this time. This section parallels what happens in real life when listeners first hear a topic or see a movie title and consider what it might be about. Learners need to learn to do this using their own resources to facilitate their listening. You can expect that the class discussion may also include consideration of some cultural norms. Make note of these ideas and consider them when you come to the cultural section of the lesson.

First Impressions

Discussing first impressions engages learners' knowledge of the world and human interaction. Students watch the video without sound and think about what might be happening. Listeners focus on some essential information such as the relationship between participants, their roles, the situation, the general topic, and the emotional tone suggested by non-verbal information. By focusing their attention on the visual context or tone-of-voice or other non-language clues, learners can begin to form hypotheses about the storyline and the characters and come to recognize that non-language information can facilitate the listening process.

Brainstorm

Brainstorming allows learners to share their conclusions and how they were formed in order to better understand the available information that permits hypothesis formation. It may encourage students to feel more comfortable to guess and help them to use their own knowledge to establish a framework.

Confirm

The strategy of confirming involves looking at more information (in this case, video with the sound on) to verify hypotheses. It also involves considering other sources of information or points that may be ambiguous and hence misleading, so in the future students can use their knowledge more effectively.

Main Idea

Once students have established a framework (through first impressions, brainstorming and confirming activities), it is much easier to establish the main idea. The questions asked in this activity are deliberately general in order to allow students to apply them to situations outside the classroom.

Predict

Predicting encourages students to use what they know about a video episode and consider what may follow — what a speaker's next sentence may be, what a listener's response may be, or what the next episode may be. Prediction is always followed by verification — watching the next episode.

Action Plan

By forming action plans, learners evaluate their use of strategies in order to employ them more effectively in the future. Students select those actions that will best facilitate their listening.

Listening for Details

Once learners have established the main idea and the framework, it is much easier to focus on the details. This strategy has students focus on getting specific information and observing details of the language functions. It appears later in the lesson to allow learners time to relax before focusing again on the demands of listening. At this point, learners watch the entire video again, focusing on content and looking for specific details and patterns of expression. The amount of detail a student can understand will naturally depend on his or her level of proficiency.

TEACHING SPEAKING/READING

The speaking and reading activities teach students how to use the specific language and language functions presented in the lesson. Students start by checking their understanding of the main issue of the lesson. They then focus on using the specific language of the lesson. Next they have an opportunity to role play the main language of the lesson. Their understanding is further solidified by the review presented in the summary. Learners then discuss differences in using these language functions between the United States and their countries. Finally, they expand their knowledge by observing and using the language in new contact situations.

Check your Understanding

In this activity, students consider what the main issue or problem of the lesson is. They look at it from the point of view of an employee and from those with whom employees may interact. They also may begin to consider some of the cultural differences that affect the issue.

interact. They also may begin to consider some of the cultural differences that affect the issue. The focus is on understanding the issues, ways to recognize the new language patterns, and functions, and circumstances under which they should use this language.

Language Skills

In the language skills activity, learners are asked to use the appropriate vocabulary and ways of expressing functions in workplace encounters. The emphasis is on breaking things into parts and beginning to produce new language.

Conversation Practice

Conversation practice enables learners to use the appropriate language in a workplace situation. They expand their understanding of the issue or problem, become more comfortable using the appropriate language, and consider variations in language use.

Summary

The summary reviews the main conversational points of the video lesson.

Cultural Exchange

In the cultural exchange, learners share information about cultural differences and gain understanding of differences in cultural behavior. Learners may also come to recognize that they are not alone in their efforts to enter and succeed in the workplace.

Contact Assignment

The contact assignment is the culminating activity of each lesson. It expands knowledge by asking students to observe examples of the issue or problem in real life situations and to consider how language may vary with the situation.

ENGLISH WORKS! — A CRITICAL INSTRUCTION PROGRAM FOR THE WORKPLACE

Many immigrants entering the workplace need help with using language in an appropriate manner. Although they may know enough English to get a job, they need to enhance their language use and listening skills to work effectively. **English Works!** provides instruction that will enable adult learners to do their work with confidence.

UNIT 1 — Interviewing for a Better Job

• •

LEARNING TO LISTEN

Thinking about the Topic

This lesson is about how to act in a job interview.

STUDENT CONVERSATION 1

First watch Student Conversation 1. Then answer these questions. Share your answers with your classmates.

1. What is a job interview?

2. What are some questions you have to answer at a job interview?

3. What are some important things to do and say at a job interview?

First Impressions

EPISODE 1

Watch Episode 1 with the sound off. Think about these questions.

1. Where are the man and the woman?

2. What is their relationship?

3. What are they talking about?

Brainstorm

Share your answers to the questions above with your classmates. Tell how you know the answers.

Confirm

Watch Episode 1 again with the sound on. Work in a small group. Review your answers to the questions above. Try to agree on the best answers. Did your answers change? What new information helped you find the best answers?

First Impressions

Watch Episode 2 with the sound off. Think about these questions.

1. Where are the man and the woman?

2. Who are they?

3. How do they feel about each other?

4. What are they talking about?

Brainstorm

Share your answers to the questions above with your classmates. Tell how you know the answers.

Main Idea

Watch Episode 2 again with the sound on. What is the main idea? Use these questions to help you find the main idea.

1. What are the man and the woman talking about?

2. Who are they talking about?

3. What problem are they discussing?

Work in a small group. Try to agree on the best answers. What new information did you get with the sound on?

First Impressions

Watch Episode 3 with the sound off. Think about these questions.

1. Where are the two women?

2. Who are they?

3. How do they feel about each other?

4. What are they talking about?

5. How does the younger woman look at the end of the episode?

Brainstorm

Share your answers to the questions above with your classmates. Tell how you know the answers.

Main Idea

Watch Episode 3 again <u>with the sound on</u>. What is the main idea? Use these questions to help you find the main idea.

     1. What are the two women talking about?

     2. What information does Phuong's supervisor give Phuong?

     3. What does Phuong think about that information?

Work in a small group. Try to agree on the best answers. What new information did you get with the sound on?

Predict

What do you think Episode 4 will be about? Why? Share your thoughts with your classmates.

Action Plan

Do you want to watch Episode 4 <u>with the sound on or off</u>? Decide with your classmates. Talk about reasons why it is helpful to have the sound on. Then talk about reasons why it is helpful to have the sound off. Make a decision.

Main Idea

Watch Episode 4 <u>with the sound on or off</u>. What is the main idea? Use these questions to help you find the main idea.

     1. Who are the two people?

     2. What is happening?

     3. What are the two people talking about?

     4. What do you think will happen?

Work in a small group. Try to agree on the best answers.

CHECK YOUR UNDERSTANDING

A. *Watch Student Conversation 2. Read the conversation between Phuong and Boju. Then answer the questions.*

BOJU: It's important to give information about yourself in an interview. You have to make the employer want to hire you.

PHUONG: Yes, you can't be shy and quiet. You have to show you are confident.

1. Was Phuong confident in her first interview with Mr. Harmon?

2. Did Phuong get the promotion after her first interview?

3. Why did you answer yes or no in question 2?

4. Have you ever had a job interview? How did you act? Did you get the job? Why or why not?

B. *Circle the correct answers to the questions about Episode 1, Phuong's first interview with Mr. Harmon.*

EXAMPLE When you are confident, you   .

    a. are fake or false, not real.

    b. tell the truth, not lies.

    (c.) are sure of yourself.

1. Phuong didn't describe her past performance. She didn't talk about:

    a. her past successes on the job.

    b. her past supervisors on the job.

    c. her past problems on the job.

2. Phuong didn't describe her qualifications or why she is qualified to do the new job. She didn't talk about:

a. the salary and the working conditions on her job.

b. any bad qualities that can cause problems on the job.

c. her job experience that makes her the best person for the job.

3. Phuong didn't discuss her career goals. Phuong made Mr. Harmon think that she wasn't thinking about the future. She didn't talk about:

a. her ideas for quitting her job to go to school.

b. her ideas for marriage and children in the future.

c. her ideas for future positions with the company.

4. It is important to ask questions about a new job. It makes the interviewer think that you are really interested in the job. A good question that Phuong did not ask is:

a. What shift will I be working?

b. Do I really have to supervise other people?

c. Why should I have to work longer hours?

C. *Circle the correct answers to the questions about Episode 4, Phuong's second interview with Mr. Harmon.*

EXAMPLE

"I am very responsible" means:

   a. I take my job seriously and do it carefully.

   b. I do exactly what I am told to do by the supervisor.

   c. I work my eight-hour shift and take long breaks.

1. Phuong says she is qualified for the job. She says:

   a. "Someday I want to study to be a nurse."

   b. "I'm very organized and responsible."

   c. "I would ask him why he's always late."

2. Phuong says her career goals are:

   a. "I was Employee of the Month."

   b. "I've had very good evaluations."

   c. "Someday I want to study to be a nurse."

3. Phuong explains how she would solve a problem on the job.

   a. "Someday I want to study to be a nurse."

   b. "I am willing to work hard."

   c. "I would tell him it's important to be on time."

4. Phuong explains some of her past successes to Mr. Harmon.

   a. "I've had very good evaluations."

   b. "I'm willing to work very hard."

   c. "Someday I want to study to be a nurse."

5. Mr. Harmon asks Phuong about a possible problem because:

   a. He thinks she can help him fix the problem.

   b. He wants to know if she is listening to him.

   c. He wants to know how she would fix the problem.

6. Phuong gives a reason why she is qualified:

    a. "I would tell him it's important to be on time."

    b. "I am willing to work hard."

    c. "I want to study."

7. Phuong presents a positive picture of herself by:

    a. giving very short answers and smiling all the time.

    b. telling about her problems with her current job.

    c. giving her qualifications and future goals.

8. Phuong describes her past performance by:

    a. talking about her awards.

    b. describing her supervisor.

    c. talking about her problems.

D. *Read the five important things to do in a job interview. Write the letter of the one that best describes each sentence.*

    a. Give job qualifications.

    b. State past performance.

    c. Give career goals.

    d. Show that you know how to solve problems.

    e. Ask questions about the new job.

EXAMPLE   "Someday I want to study to be a nurse." _____*C*_____

1. ". . . and I got a thank-you letter for the extra work I did." _____

2. "If we had a leak in a sink, I would shut down the water and check the seals and the pipes." _____

3. "Could you tell me how many housekeepers I would supervise?" _____

4. "My current work includes organizing the inventory system and teaching all the employees the new system." _____

5. "I'm very responsible and I always come early to work." _____

LANGUAGE SKILLS

Read the conversation between Phuong and Mr. Harmon from Episode 4, the second interview.

MR. HARMON: Why do you think you're qualified for this position?

PHUONG: I am very organized and responsible. I am willing to work hard.

MR. HARMON: What if an employee comes in late all the time. What would you do as supervisor?

PHUONG: I would ask him why he is always late. I would tell him it is important to be on time.

MR. HARMON: Why do you deserve a promotion at this time?

PHUONG: I've had very good evaluations; I was Employee of the Month.

MR. HARMON: What are your career goals?

PHUONG: Someday I want to study to be a nurse.

Find four questions Mr. Harmon asks Phuong. These are important in any job interview. Write them here.

1. _____

2. _____

3. _____

4. _____

Which question asks about:

career goals	1	2	3	4
solving problems	1	2	3	4
qualifications	1	2	3	4
past performance	1	2	3	4

LISTENING FOR DETAILS

Watch all the episodes again with the sound on. Answer these questions. Share your answers with your classmates.

1. Does Mr. Harmon ask Phuong about:

	FIRST INTERVIEW	SECOND INTERVIEW
her career goals		
solving problems		
her qualifications		
her past performance		
any questions about the new job		

2. How does Phuong answer these questions in the *first interview*?

3. What specific advice does Phuong's supervisor give her?

4. How does Phuong answer these questions in the *second interview*?

CONVERSATION PRACTICE

Work with a partner. Read the following situations. Student A is the interviewer and Student B is an employee who is applying for a new position. Student A, write out questions to ask the employee. The interview should include:

- the applicant's past experiences
- the applicant's job qualifications
- the applicant's future career plans
- how the applicant would handle a problem on the job
- any questions the applicant has

Then role-play the interviews with your partner. Take turns as the interviewer.

1. **Situation:** The applicant is a housekeeper in a hotel and is applying for the job of supervisor.

2. **Situation:** The applicant is a maintenance assistant in a large company and is applying for a position as a maintenance engineer.

3. **Situation:** Make up your own interview. Decide on the roles of the interviewer and the employee. What position is the employee applying for?

Summary

Watch the Summary Presentation. Then read the summary below. Discuss any questions you have about Interviewing for a Better Job with your teacher and classmates.

When you interview for a better job, it is important to make a good impression.

Be prepared to:

- answer questions
- give reasons why you are qualified
- document your past performance
- describe your career plans
- ask a question about the new job
- discuss how you would deal with problems

Work with a partner. Share information about a time you had an interview. What questions did the interviewer ask you? What did you answer?

CULTURAL EXCHANGE

Discuss these questions. Share your answers with your classmates.

1. Compare the way Phuong behaves in the first and second interview with Mr. Harmon. How is she sitting? Does she look Mr. Harmon in the eye? Is she confident?

2. What do American employers think of employees who are quiet and don't look them in the eye?

3. What kind of posture (the way a person sits) do Americans expect their employees to have?

4. When employees in your country want a new job, do they have an interview?

5. If they have an interview:

   • What is the best way to make a good impression?
   • How should employees answer questions about themselves?
   • How should employees answer questions about the new job?
   • Should an employee ask questions about the new job?
   • What kind of posture and eye contact do employers in your country expect their employees to have?

CONTACT ASSIGNMENT

A. Write a response to the following interview questions for a promotion for yourself. Include as much positive information as possible. Share your answers with your classmates.

1. Why would you make a good supervisor?

_____

_____

_____

2. What would you do if you had a problem with your workers taking long lunch breaks?

_____

_____

_____

3. What have you done in other jobs that would help you do the new job well?

_____

_____

_____

4. What do you plan to do professionally in the future? How do you plan to do this?

_____

_____

_____

B. Interview a friend, your teacher, or your supervisor. Ask him or her about a job interview he or she had. What questions did the interviewer ask. Write the questions here. Share your questions with your classmates.

_____

_____

_____

Asking for Elaboration of a Request or Order

LEARNING TO LISTEN

Thinking about the Topic

If you don't understand someone at work, it is important to ask for more information. This lesson is about asking for more information.

STUDENT

CONVERSATION 1

First watch Student Conversation 1. Then answer these questions. Share your answers with your classmates.

1. Your boss asks you to do something, but you are not sure you understand. What should you do?

2. What can you say if you need more information?

3. Why should you ask for more information, especially at work?

First Impressions

Watch Episode 1 with the sound off. Think about these questions.

1. Where are the women?

2. What is the relationship between the first two women?

3. Who is the third woman who comes in?

4. What is her relationship to the two women?

5. What happens in Episode 1?

Brainstorm

Share your answers to the questions above with your classmates. Tell how you know the answers.

Main Idea

Watch Episode 1 again <u>with the sound on</u>. What is the main idea? Use these questions to help you find the main idea.

> **1.** What are the first two women talking about?
>
> **2.** What is the problem?
>
> **3.** What does the third woman do about the problem?

Work in a small group. Try to agree on the best answers. What new information did you get with the sound on?

Predict

What do you think Episode 2 will be about? Why? Share your thoughts with your classmates.

First Impressions

Watch Episode 2 <u>with the sound off</u>. Think about these questions.

> **1.** Where are the two women?
>
> **2.** What is their relationship?
>
> **3.** What are they talking about?
>
> **4.** How does the younger woman feel?

Brainstorm

Share your answers to the questions above with your classmates. Tell how you know the answers.

Main Idea

Watch Episode 2 again <u>with the sound on</u>. What is the main idea? Use these questions to help you find the main idea.

> **1.** What is the problem?
>
> **2.** What caused the problem?
>
> **3.** What can be done to avoid the problem?

Work in a small group. Try to agree on the best answers. What new information did you get with the sound on?

STUDENT

CONVERSATION 2

Watch Student Conversation 2 with the sound on. Discuss these questions. Share your answers with your classmates.

1. What does Boju say?

2. Does Maria agree?

3. Why is it important to ask for more information?

4. Is it difficult to ask for more information sometimes? Why?

5. Do you sometimes ask for more information? Give an example.

6. Did you ever make a mistake because you didn't ask for more information? When?

Main Idea

EPISODE 3

Watch Episode 3 with the sound on. What is the main idea? Use these questions to help you find the main idea.

1. Where are the two people?

2. Who are they?

3. What are they talking about?

4. What is the problem?

Work in a small group. Try to agree on the best answers.

Main Idea

EPISODE 4

Watch Episode 4 with the sound on. What is the main idea? Use these questions to help you find the main idea.

1. Where are the two people?

2. Who are they?

3. What are they talking about?

4. What is the problem?

Work in a small group. Try to agree on the best answers.

STUDENT
CONVERSATION 3

Watch Student Conversation 3 with the sound on. Discuss these questions. Share your answers with your classmates.

1. Does Maria understand why it is important to understand instructions?

2. Do you think that Maria will ask for more information now?

3. Why does Boju say that it is important to ask for more information?

CHECK YOUR UNDERSTANDING

A. *Read the conversation between Mrs. Madison and Maria. Then answer the questions.*

Mrs. Madison asked Maria to clean her room. Maria has just finished cleaning Mrs. Madison's room. She picked up all the trash around the chair. Mrs. Madison comes back into the the room and is looking for something.

MRS. MADISON: I forgot my letter. Did you find a letter?

MARIA: Well, there were some old papers and old tissues on the floor. I was sure they were trash. Nothing looked very important.

MRS. MADISON: Oh no, you should have asked me.

Mrs. Madison begins to cry as she realizes the letter is gone.

1. Was Mrs. Madison sad? Why?

2. Was she angry with Maria? Why?

3. Why did Mrs. Madison lose her letter?

4. What did Mrs. Madison think Maria should do?

5. In order to do a good job, what did Maria need to know?

6. Have you ever made a mistake like this? Tell your classmates.

B. *Read the information in the box. Then circle the correct answers.*

Asking for elaboration means you ask for more information. You ask for elaboration to be sure you completely understand a request or an order. Then you don't have to guess.

EXAMPLE   Asking for elaboration is:

    a. guessing what someone means.

    b. asking someone to repeat something because you didn't hear it.

    c. asking for more information.

1. Maria made a mistake because:

    a. she didn't call her supervisor.

    b. she didn't ask Mrs. Madison about the papers on the floor.

    c. she didn't clean carefully under the bed and around the chair.

2. Mrs. Madison thinks that:

    a. Maria should not have cleaned the room.

    b. Maria should not have picked up the trash on the floor.

    c. Maria should not have thrown away the papers without asking.

3. You ask for elaboration when:

    a. you want your supervisor to give you more work.

    b. you want your supervisor to give the meaning of a word.

    c. you want your supervisor to give you more details.

4. Asking for elaboration will help you:

    a. understand the speaker and the instructions.

    b. be sure the speaker understands you.

    c. be clear about what the speaker means.

5. When your supervisor gives you an order that is not clear to you, you should:

    a. keep quiet and do the job.

    b. say nothing and ask a co-worker.

    c. ask the supervisor to give you more information.

C. *Read the information in the box. Then circle the correct answer.*

> It is important to ask for elaboration when you need to know:
>
> - who is responsible for the job
> - where the tools or materials are
> - what tools you need
> - what steps you need to take to do the job
> - who can help if you have a question
> - what time to start (or finish) the job
>
> You need to think about the job from beginning to end. Do you understand everything about doing that job? If you need more details or specific information, be sure to ask for it.

1. When someone gives you an order, you should:

    a. try to understand what he or she said later when you are alone.

    b. think about the job from start to finish and ask questions.

    c. ask your supervisor to repeat everything another time.

2. When you aren't sure what tools you need to do a job, ask:

    a. When should I get the tools from the box?

    b. What tools do I need?

    c. Where are the tools I need?

3. When you don't know exactly where to go to do the job, ask:

    a. When do I need to do the job?

    b. Where do I need to do the job?

    c. Why do I need to do the job?

4. When you don't know the person responsible for the job, ask:

   a. Who should I ask about it?

   b. When should I ask about it?

   c. Where should I ask about it?

5. When you don't know when to start (or finish) the job, ask:

   a. Where is the job?

   b. What time do I need to start (or finish)?

   c. What tools do I need?

D. *It is important to get all the information before you begin a job. Circle all the reasons why it is important to ask for elaboration.*

   1. to avoid mistakes

   2. to impress your supervisor

   3. to give better service

   4. to practice your English

   5. to keep a conversation going

   6. to prevent mistakes

   7. to prevent accidents

   8. to waste time

   9. to save time by doing the job right the first time

   10. to impress your friends

Discuss your answers with your classmates. Do you all agree?

LANGUAGE SKILLS

A. *Read the information in the box.*

> You can ask several kinds of questions to get more information. These include **who**, **what**, **where**, **when**, and **how** questions. For example:
>
> - Who should I help first?
> - What time should I finish painting?
> - Where would you like to go?
> - When do you want it delivered?
> - How do you want your coffee?

The sentences below are orders or requests that are given on the job. Match the sentences with the best questions to ask.

EXAMPLE

1. Please take Mrs. Madison for a walk outside.

   _____2_____ a. cleaner should I use?

2. Clean it up.

   _____1_____ b. **Where** should we go?

Part A

1. I want to buy a lottery ticket.

   _____ a. **Where** is that office?

2. You have to get a parking permit in the main office.

   _____ b. **How long** will you be staying, sir?

3. Take the bleach and clean that tile in the bathroom.

   _____ c. **What kind** do you want?

4. Please fold all the towels and sheets in this basket.

   _____ d. **Which** bottle do I use? There's no label.

5. I want a hotel suite.

   _____ e. **When** does it need to be done?

Part B

6. I'm going on vacation soon. You'll be the supervisor while I'm away.

_____ f. **How many** cartons of snacks are there?

7. You have to get this done this afternoon.

_____ g. **When** do you plan to go?

8. I'm lost. Can you help me find this place?

_____ h. **Who** do I need to see?

9. I don't know. Check with someone in the office.

_____ i. **What time** do you need it finished?

10. Put the snacks on that shelf.

_____ j. **Where** do you need to go?

B. *Read the information in the box.*

> Sometimes you need to ask a yes/no or choice question to get more information. For example:
>
> • Is the box you want in the closet?
> • Do you want the green sweater?
> • Do you want me to throw these papers away or put them on your desk?

For each order or request below write a yes/no or choice question to ask for more elaboration.

EXAMPLE

Please bring me the notebook.

Do you want the red one or the blue one?

1. Please bring me that book over there.

_____

2. I need something to drink, please.

_____

3. I'm cold. Can you do something about it?

_____

4. Be sure to clean the rooms.

_____

5. Can you give me some paper, please?

_____

6. I want some eggs.

_____

7. Two pounds of onions, please.

_____

8. A cup of coffee, please.

_____

9. Please bring me a towel.

_____

10. Watch out for that wire!

_____

C. *Look at each picture and read each dialogue. Circle the letter of the most appropriate question.*

EXAMPLE

Ms. Williams: I want you to take Mrs. Madison for a walk.

Boju: I'd be happy to do that. _____ ?

    a. Why do you want me to do that?

    b. Who do you want me to take?

    c. What time do you want me to do it?

1. Boju is taking Mrs. Madison out for her afternoon walk.

Mrs. Madison: Boju, thank you for taking me out this afternoon. I can't wait to get some fresh air.

Boju: Oh, it's always a pleasure to walk with you, Mrs. Madison. Now that we're out of the room, _____ ?

    a. when would you like to go?

    b. where would you like to go?

    c. why do you want to go?

2. Ms. Williams: Don't forget Mrs. Madison must get back for her medicine.

Boju: That's no problem. _____ ?

    a. Why does she need to go for a walk?

    b. Where do I take her?

    c. What time does she need to take it?

3. Maria: I picked up a lot of things from the floor today.

Mrs. Madison: Oh, really?

Maria: Yes, and I found this letter. _____ ?

    a. What do you want me to do with it?

    b. Can I read it?

    c. Who would want such an old letter?

LISTENING FOR DETAILS

Watch all the episodes again with the sound on. Answer these questions.

1. Count the number of examples of elaboration in each episode. Write the number here. Compare your results with your classmates.

   Episode 1 _____   **Episode 3** _____

   Episode 2 _____   **Episode 4** _____

2. Listen for one example of elaboration. Write it here. Share your example with your classmates.

CONVERSATION PRACTICE

Work with a partner. Student A makes a request. Student B asks for more information. Then switch roles. Role-play your conversations for your classmates.

EXAMPLE
Situation: Restaurant
Student A: Waiter/Waitress
Student B: Cook

Waiter/Waitress: I need 3 eggs with bacon.
Cook: How do you want the eggs cooked?

---

1. Situation: 7-Eleven Store
   Student A: Customer
   Student B: Clerk

2. Situation: Department Store
   Student A: Supervisor gives orders
   Student B: Clerk

3. Situation: Hospital
   Student A: Patient
   Student B: Nurse

4. Situation: Hotel
   Student A: Maintenance Worker
   Student B: Boss

5. Situation: Restaurant
   Student A: Cashier
   Student B: Customer

6. Situation: Restaurant
   Student A: Waiter/Waitress
   Student B: Customer

CULTURAL EXCHANGE

Read the conversation between Maria and Boju.

BOJU: You know, Maria, you just have to ask questions to make sure you really understand.

MARIA: Yes. I thought it was impolite. I just followed instructions and didn't ask questions.

BOJU: Yes, I know. But here in America it's important to ask for more information. You have to do that so you don't make so many mistakes and make people angry. I've learned that whenever people ask me to do something or give me an order, I always ask for more information.

Discuss these questions. Share your answers with your classmates.

1. Why didn't Maria ask questions?

2. Boju gives two reasons why it is important to ask for more information. What are they?

3. Is it polite to ask questions of a supervisor in your country?

4. If you don't ask for elaboration in your country, how do you understand what to do?

SUMMARY

Watch the Summary Presentation. Then read the summary below. Discuss any questions you have about Asking for Elaboration with your teacher and classmates.

When you get instructions, think about what other information you need to know. Then, ask questions. When you get instructions, you may need more information, so ask more questions. When you ask more questions, you get more information, and you do a better job.

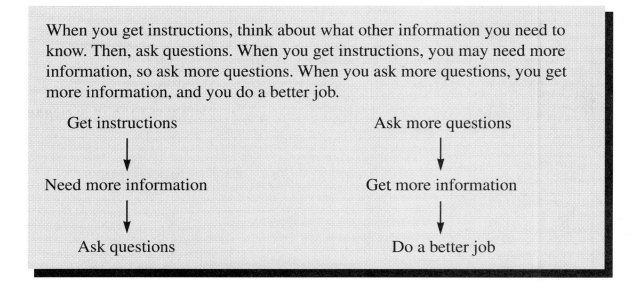

Get instructions

↓

Need more information

↓

Ask questions

Ask more questions

↓

Get more information

↓

Do a better job

CONTACT ASSIGNMENT

A. Make a list of all the question words you can remember from this lesson. (If you can't remember them all, look through the lesson.)

_____   _____   _____

_____   _____   _____

_____   _____   _____

B. Practice asking questions to get more information at work or at school. When your supervisor or your teacher gives an instruction, think of at least one question you can ask to get more information. Write the question down.

1. Supervisor's or teacher's instruction:

_____

_____

Your question:

_____

_____

2. Supervisor's or teacher's instruction:

_____

_____

Your question:

_____

_____

Share your questions with your classmates. Can they think of other questions to get more information?

Dealing with Mistakes

• •

LEARNING TO LISTEN

Thinking about the Topic

This lesson is about apologizing.

STUDENT

CONVERSATION 1

First watch Student Conversation 1. Then answer these questions. Share your answers with your classmates.

1. What is an apology?

2. When should you apologize?

3. Why is it important to apologize?

First Impressions

EPISODE 1

Watch Episode 1 with the sound off. Think about these questions.

1. Where are the three people?

2. Who are they?

3. What are they talking about?

4. How do they feel about one another?

Brainstorm

Share your answers to the questions above with your classmates. Tell how you know the answers.

Main Idea

Watch Episode 1 again with the sound on. What is the main idea? Use these questions to help you find the main idea.

> **1.** What is the problem in Episode 1?
>
> **2.** How does the clerk deal with the problem? What does she say?
>
> **3.** Does the older man solve the problem? How?

Work in a small group. Try to agree on the best answers. What new information did you get with the sound on?

STUDENT

CONVERSATION 2

Watch Student Conversation 2 with the sound on. Discuss these questions. Share your answers with your classmates.

> **1.** Why doesn't Phuong want to apologize?
>
> **2.** Who does Aakhu apologize to?
>
> **3.** Tell about a time when you made a mistake and apologized to someone. How did you feel?
>
> **4.** Tell about a time when you made a mistake but didn't apologize. How did you feel then?

Predict

What do you think Episode 2 will be about? Why? Share your thoughts with your classmates.

First Impressions

Watch Episode 2 with the sound off. Think about these questions.

> **1.** Where are the three people?
>
> **2.** Who are they?
>
> **3.** How do they feel about one another?
>
> **4.** What are they talking about?

Brainstorm

Share your answers to the questions above with your classmates. Tell how you know the answers.

Main Idea

Watch Episode 2 again with the sound on. What is the main idea? Use these questions to help you find the main idea.

1. What is the problem in Episode 2?

2. What does the woman clerk do about it?

3. What does the man clerk do? What does he say?

Work in a small group. Try to agree on the best answers. What new information did you get with the sound on?

Main Idea

Watch Episode 3 with the sound on. What is the main idea? Use these questions to help you find the main idea.

1. Who are the people?

2. What are they talking about?

3. What is the problem?

4. Do they solve the problem? How?

Work in a small group. Try to agree on the best answers.

Action Plan

Do you want to watch Episode 4 with the sound on or off? Decide with your classmates. Talk about reasons why it is helpful to have the sound on. Then talk about reasons why it is helpful to have the sound off. Make a decision.

Main Idea

Watch Episode 4 with the sound on or off. What is the main idea? Use these questions to help you find the main idea.

1. Who are the people?

2. What does the man say?

3. What is the problem?

4. How is the problem solved?

Work in a small group. Try to agree on the best answers.

STUDENT

CONVERSATION 3

Watch Student Conversation 3 with the sound on. Discuss these questions. Share your answers with your classmates.

1. Who should apologize?

2. Does Phuong agree?

3. Tell about a time when someone made a mistake and apologized to you.

4. Tell about a time when someone made a mistake and didn't apologize to you. How did you feel then?

CHECK YOUR UNDERSTANDING

A. *Read the conversation between Phuong and Mr. White from Episode 1.*

PHUONG: I gave his room to someone else by mistake. I didn't tell him. I thought it would be bad to say I made a mistake.

MR. WHITE: It is better to apologize for a mistake, explain what happened, and correct the problem.

Mr. White gives three steps to apologizing. Write them here.

1. _____

2. _____

3. _____

When you make a mistake, it's important to apologize immediately. You should:

    1. Apologize: Say you are sorry.

    2. Explain: Say *why* you made the mistake. Say why there was a problem.

    3. Correct: Offer to fix the problem.

B. *Circle the correct answer.*

EXAMPLE   Apologizing is:

    a. telling someone what happened.

    b. telling someone that you didn't do anything wrong.

    c. telling someone that you are sorry.

1. Phuong didn't say anything to the guest about the mistake because:

   a. She didn't care what the guest thought.

   b. She thought it was wrong to tell about her mistake.

   c. She was afraid of being fired.

2. The *first* thing you should do when you make a mistake is:

   a. keep quiet and try to fix it right away.

   b. apologize to the person.

   c. find your supervisor and ask him or her to apologize.

3. An explanation is part of an apology. You should:

   a. say that someone else did it.

   b. try to fix the problem right away.

   c. tell the person how and why the mistake happened.

4. After you apologize and explain, you should:

   a. say who is responsible for the problem.

   b. try to fix the problem immediately.

   c. say that you are sorry two more times.

5. Which one is an explanation:

   a. It's not my fault!

   b. I'm sorry.

   c. The bus was late.

C. *Read the conversation between Aakhu and Mike from Episode 2.*

AAKHU: Oh, the computer is down. I can't give you your tickets right now.

MIKE: What do you mean? I've been waiting in line for ten minutes. *Now* you tell me the computer is down?

AAKHU: There is nothing I can do about it. You'll have to wait. It's not my fault.

Circle the correct answers. If you are not sure, remember when you apologize you should:

1. Apologize

2. Explain

3. Correct

EXAMPLE   "It's not my fault" means:

a. I didn't make the mistake.

b. It's not my problem.

c. It's not my apology.

1. Aakhu says "It's not my fault" because:

a. She doesn't like the customer.

b. She didn't cause the computer problem.

c. She doesn't like the job.

2. The customer is angry because:

a. He has been waiting ten minutes.

b. Aakhu has been very rude to him.

c. He doesn't like computers.

3. The first thing Aakhu forgot was to:

   a. explain the computer problem.

   b. apologize to the customer.

   c. offer free coffee.

4. It's important to make a customer feel comfortable because:

   a. the customer will make you feel better too.

   b. the customer will be your friend.

   c. you want the customer to come back to your store.

5. In the United States it is the custom to:

   a. get angry with customers in stores.

   b. apologize whenever there is a problem.

   c. look away when someone is angry with you.

D. *Read the conversation between Mike and James from Episode 2.*

MIKE: Well, I don't see it that way. Because of this, I'm going to be late getting back to work! You're not going to be seeing me here anymore.

JAMES: We're sorry, sir, but the computer is down. I know you're in a hurry but it should be back up in a few minutes. If you want to wait, we can give you a cup of coffee or a soda.

MIKE: OK. I'll wait a few minutes. Where's the coffee?

Find the three parts of the apology in the conversation. Write them here.

apology _____

explanation _____

correction _____

E. *The following employees have made mistakes on the job. Read the conversations and put an X in the box under the part(s) of an apology they include.*

If they include all three parts, put an X under **complete**. *If they are missing a part, put an X under* **incomplete**.

EXAMPLE

Mr. Jones: I made a reservation for a room with a double bed. I didn't get one.

Mr. White: There's been a mix-up in your reservation.

APOLOGY	EXPLANATION	CORRECTION	COMPLETE	INCOMPLETE
	X			X

Mr. White's answer is incomplete. He didn't give an apology or offer a correction to the situation. He did give an explanation by telling Mr. Jones that there had been a mix-up.

1. James: Aakhu, could you get me a couple of chocolate donuts and some napkins for this woman, please?

(Aakhu gives the donuts to James.)

James: Oh, and some napkins *too*.

Aakhu: Uh-oh, I forgot. Here you are.

APOLOGY	EXPLANATION	CORRECTION	COMPLETE	INCOMPLETE

2. Mr. Jones: I made a reservation for a room with a double bed. I didn't get one. The new room is more expensive! You can be sure I'll never come back to this hotel again.

Mr. White: Mr. Jones, I apologize for the inconvenience. There's been a mix-up in your reservation. You may have a better room at no extra charge. Here is the key. Again, I'm very sorry.

APOLOGY	EXPLANATION	CORRECTION	COMPLETE	INCOMPLETE

3. Mr. Jones: I ordered a ham sandwich and Room Service brought up a turkey sandwich. You have to take that off my bill.

Phuong: Certainly, sir. I'm very sorry about the mistake, Mr. Jones. I'll call Room Service and order you a ham sandwich right away. There will be no charge, sir.

APOLOGY	EXPLANATION	CORRECTION	COMPLETE	INCOMPLETE

4. James accidentally knocks Aakhu against the pizza oven.

Aakhu: Ouch! I just burned my thumb. What happened?

James: Oh Aakhu, I slipped on this water over here and accidentally pushed you. I'll go get the first aid kit. You sit down over there.

APOLOGY	EXPLANATION	CORRECTION	COMPLETE	INCOMPLETE

LISTENING FOR DETAILS

Watch all the episodes again with the sound on. Answer these questions.

1. Count the number of apologies in each episode. Write the number here. Compare your results with your classmates.

   Episode 1 _____   **Episode 3** _____

   Episode 2 _____   **Episode 4** _____

2. Listen for one example of an apology. Write it here. Share your example with your classmates.

   _____

   _____

LANGUAGE SKILLS

Work with a partner. Practice giving an apology and an explanation. Take turns.

EXAMPLE   Roles: Store Clerk and Customer

The store clerk is helping one customer. Another customer comes over to buy something and interrupts. The store clerk apologizes.

Customer: Can you help me, please?

Store Clerk: I'm sorry. I'm with another customer.

1. Roles: Two Workers

Worker 1 cleared a lunch table in order to eat there and threw part of a sandwich into the trash. He or she thought the person had finished. Worker 2 comes back looking for his or her sandwich. Worker 1 apologizes and gives an explanation.

Worker 2: Where's my sandwich?

Worker 1: _____

2. Roles: Supervisor and Employee

The supervisor didn't tell an employee that there was a meeting last night. The supervisor thought the employee already knew about it. The employee is very unhappy. The supervisor apologizes and gives an explanation.

Employee: I didn't go to the meeting last night. No one told me about it.

Supervisor:_____

3. Roles: Waiter/Waitress and Customer

There was an emergency in the kitchen. So, by the time the waiter/waitress brought the food to the customer it was cold. The customer complains. The waiter/waitress apologizes and gives an explanation.

Customer: My food is cold.

Waiter/Waitress: _____

4. Roles: Clerk and Customer

The customer asked for ten airmail stamps. The postal clerk didn't hear the word *airmail* and gave the customer ten regular stamps. The clerk apologizes and gives an explanation.

Customer: I asked for ten airmail stamps.

Clerk: _____

5. Roles: Waiter/Waitress and Customer

The customer asks for chicken. The restaurant doesn't have any more. The waiter/waitress apologizes and gives an explanation.

Customer: I'll take the chicken.

Waiter/Waitress: _____

CONVERSATION PRACTICE

Work with a partner. Read the situations and practice making complete apologies. Remember to include an apology, an explanation, and a correction. Then choose one role play to perform for the class.

1. Roles: Worker and Chief of Security

   Situation: A worker has just lost his or her keys to the building. The worker knows that the company is very concerned about security. The worker goes to see the chief of security in the building.

2. Roles: Worker and Supervisor

   Situation: A worker went to the store for the supervisor but forgot to get one of the things on the list.

3. Roles: Worker and Supervisor

   Situation: A worker was supposed to finish a job during his or her shift, but didn't finish it. The worker had to fix a maintenance problem that took three hours.

4. Roles: Worker and Supervisor

   Situation: A worker made a mistake on the daily inventory and didn't realize the mistake until after he or she got home. The worker calls back to the office to talk to the supervisor.

5. Roles: Two Workers

   Situation: Worker 1 asks Worker 2 to help out by switching shifts tomorrow. Worker 2 can't because of plans to help his or her older mother move.

Summary

Watch the Summary Presentation. Then read the summary below. Discuss any questions you have about Dealing with Mistakes with your teacher and classmates.

When you make a mistake, it's important to say you're sorry. When you make a mistake:

- Apologize: "I'm sorry."
- Give a reason for the problem, if possible: "I didn't understand."
- Offer to correct the problem.

When you can't correct the problem immediately or if it was a big mistake, companies often offer something extra. Companies will usually tell you what else to give.

Apologies are important in the United States.

CULTURAL EXCHANGE

Read Student Conversation 2.

PHUONG: In our culture, we are sometimes ashamed when we make a mistake. So, we don't say anything.

AAKHU: But here, people want to hear you apologize. It is the custom. I try to do that with everyone: customers, co-workers, and supervisors. One time I didn't, and the customer got really mad.

Phuong is worried about admitting that she made a mistake. Aakhu says that it is important to say you're sorry. Discuss these questions. Share your answers with` your classmates.

1. What do people do when they make a mistake in your country?

2. Do people apologize? When? What do they say?

3. How do you feel about apologizing in the United States? Is it easy or difficult? Why?

CONTACT ASSIGNMENT

A. Think about some mistakes you might make at work (or at school or at home). Think about how you could apologize. Share your thoughts with your classmates. Brainstorm what you might say.

B. Listen for apologies at work (or at school). Listen for apologies that include an apology, an explanation, and a correction. Write down one complete apology you hear.

apology: _____

explanation: _____

correction: _____

C. You made a mistake at work (or at school). Describe the actions you took. Did you apologize, explain the mistake, and correct it? What did you say? Tell your classmates. You can write notes here.

_____

_____

_____

_____

_____

_____

D. Go to a hotel or a restaurant in your city. Interview an employee. Ask if the company gives something extra (like a cup of coffee or a bottle of wine) if an employee makes a mistake. Share your information with your classmates.

UNIT 4 Reading Job Announcements

LEARNING TO LISTEN

Thinking about the Topic

This lesson is about why it is important to read job announcements carefully.

STUDENT

CONVERSATION 1

First watch Student Conversation 1. Then answer these questions. Share your answers with your classmates.

1. How do you know when a company has a job opening?

2. What does a job announcement tell you?

3. Where do you find job announcements?

4. How do you know if you should apply for a job?

First Impressions

EPISODE 1

Watch Episode 1 with the sound off. Think about these questions.

1. Where are the four men?

2. Who are they?

3. What is their relationship?

4. What are they talking about?

Brainstorm

Share your answers to the questions above with your classmates. Tell how you know the answers.

Confirm

Watch Episode 1 again with the sound on. Work in a small group. Review your answers to the questions above. Try to agree on the best answers. Did your answers change? What new information helped you find the best answers?

First Impressions

Watch Episode 2 with the sound off. Think about these questions.

1. What is the relationship between the first three men?

2. How do they feel about one another?

3. What are the three men talking about?

4. What is the fourth man saying to the man who is sleeping or dreaming?

Brainstorm

Share your answers to the questions above with your classmates. Tell how you know the answers.

Main Idea

Watch Episode 2 again with the sound on. What is the main idea? Use these questions to help you find the main idea.

1. How does the man in white behave?

2. How does he speak to the other two men? What does he say?

3. Is this a dream? How do you know?

4. How does the episode end?

Work in a small group. Try to agree on the best answers. What new information did you get with the sound on?

Main Idea

Watch Episode 3 with the sound on. What is the main idea? Use these questions to help you find the main idea.

1. What is the man looking at?

2. What is he filling out?

3. What do you think he is going to do next ?

Work in a small group. Try to agree on the best answers.

Predict

What do you think Episode 4 will be about? Why? Share your thoughts with your classmates.

Action Plan

Do you want to watch Episode 4 with the sound on or off? Decide with your classmates. Talk about reasons why it is helpful to have the sound on. Then talk about reasons why it is helpful to have the sound off. Make a decision.

Main Idea

Watch Episode 4 with the sound on or off. What is the main idea? Use these questions to help you find the main idea.

1. Who are the two people?

2. What is their relationship?

3. What are they talking about?

4. How does the episode end?

Work in a small group. Try to agree on the best answers.

STUDENT

CONVERSATION 2

Watch Student Conversation 2 with the sound on. Discuss these questions. Share your answers with your classmates.

1. Why was Boju embarrassed?

2. Did he read the job announcement?

3. Have you ever applied for a job? Tell about your experience.

First Impressions

Watch Episode 5 with the sound off. Think about these questions.

1. Where are the two women?

2. Who are they?

3. What are they talking about?

Brainstorm

Share your answers to the questions above with your classmates. Tell how you know the answers.

Main Idea

Watch Episode 5 again with the sound on. What is the main idea? Use these questions to help you find the main idea.

1. What are Maria and Phuong talking about?

2. What does Aakhu say?

3. What does Maria decide? Why?

Work in a small group. Try to agree on the best answers. What new information did you get with the sound on?

STUDENT

CONVERSATION 3

Watch Student Conversation 3 with the sound on. Discuss these questions. Share your answers with your classmates.

1. Does Maria think that it is important to read the job announcement? Why?

2. Does Boju plan to read the job announcement next time?

CHECK YOUR UNDERSTANDING

A. *Read the conversation from Episode 4. Then answer the questions.*

MR. JONES: What is your experience in maintenance?

BOJU: I do all the maintenance at my house. I have a lot of experience in maintenance.

MR. JONES: This job requires three years' experience in hospital maintenance.

BOJU: I'm sure I can do it.

MR. JONES: How long have you worked at this hospital?

BOJU: Two months.

MR. JONES: (impatiently) You have to be here at least one year to be a supervisor. Didn't you read the requirements for the job?

1. What are two requirements or qualifications Boju needs for the job. Write them here.

   a. _____

   _____

   b _____

   _____

2. Is Mr. Jones angry? Why?

3. If Boju had read the job announcement, do you think he would have applied? If no, why not?

4. Have you ever applied for a job you were not qualified for? When?

B. *Read the definition and match the job title with the correct job description.*

JOB TITLE is the name of a job.

1. housekeeper   _____ a. gives medicine

2. maintenance supervisor   _____ b. works at a counter

3. 7-Eleven clerk   _____ c. makes beds

4. nurse   _____ d. manages custodians

5. custodian   _____ e. delivers letters

6. teacher   _____ f. fixes machines

7. mail carrier   _____ g. prepares food

8. cafeteria worker   _____ h. helps students

C. *Read the definitions and circle the correct answer.*

JOB QUALIFICATIONS or JOB REQUIREMENTS are the skills and experience you need to do the job. For example: Ability to type 50 words per minute. Ability to work with people from many cultures.

1. Which one is a job qualification:

   a. custodian

   b. starts July 1

   c. knows how to make up a schedule

2. Which one is a job qualification:

   a. apply before July 1

   b. gets along well with people

   c. nurse

3. Which one is a job qualification:

   a. maintenance supervisor

   b. prepares food

   c. must be very organized

> **JOB DUTIES, JOB DESCRIPTION, JOB RESPONSIBILITY, or JOB SUMMARY** tells what you will do on the job. For example: clean the room, fix equipment.

4. Which one is a job description:

   a. custodian

   b. makes beds

   c. nice person

5. Which one is a job description:

   a. cafeteria worker

   b. two years experience as a supervisor

   c. organizes work schedules

> **STARTING DATE** is the day you begin a new job.

6. Which one is the starting date:

   a. day shift

   b. begins on December 1

   c. after 3 P.M.

7. Which one is the starting date:

   a. apply before June 1

   b. part time

   c. needed immediately

WHERE TO APPLY tells you the location to go to.

8. Which one tells you where to apply:

   a. see Ms. Brown

   b. bring your driver's license

   c. apply after October 1

9. Which one tells you where to apply:

   a. apply in person

   b. apply in personnel

   c. apply with references

HOURLY WAGE tells how much you will earn per hour.

10. Which one describes the hourly wage for the job:

   a. $20,000 annual salary

   b. $5.00 per hour

   c. part time

D. *Answer the questions. Discuss your answers with your classmates.*

1. How do you know what abilities and experience are required for a new job?

2. When should you read a job announcement?

3. What are two reasons why it helps to read a job announcement?

LANGUAGE SKILLS

Each of the job announcements below has five parts. Identify the parts of the job announcements. Write the part next to each number. These are the parts.

job title

job qualifications

job duties

starting date

where to apply

EXAMPLE

1. _____ *job title* _____

HOUSEKEEPER

2. _____ *qualifications* _____

Work in hospital housekeeping department for nine months or more

Able to communicate well

Able to pass test of skill and mechanical aptitude to determine equipment problems

Able to use chemicals and equipment for cleaning

Able to get along well with co-workers, supervisors, and patients

3. _____ *duties* _____

Clean and supply patient rooms, nurses' stations, bathrooms

Use cleaning tools and all products and supplies

Make daily written report on work

4. _____ *where to apply* _____

Personnel Office

5. _____ *starting date* _____

Immediately

Now identify the parts of a job announcement in the following three examples.

JOB ANNOUNCEMENT 1

1. _____

ENVIRONMENTAL SERVICES WORKER

2. _____

Daily sweeping and mopping of all floor space, basement, and other public areas

Occasional waxing of all floor space and basement

Daily removal of trash and cleaning of trash rooms

Window cleaning, furniture dusting, cleaning of window blinds, and cleaning and polishing of elevators

Snow and ice removal, as required

3. _____

Must have at least one year of floor care experience

Must be able to work independently within general rules established by supervisor

Must be thoroughly familiar with the proper use and maintenance of all equipment used

Must be able to read, write, speak, and follow written and oral instructions in English as necessary to accomplish job

4. _____

Immediately or as soon as possible

5. _____

In the front office

JOB ANNOUNCEMENT 2

1. _____

STORE CLERK

2. _____

    Operate cash register and correctly make change

    Answer customer questions about location of products

    Sell donuts, cigarettes, and lottery tickets

    Prepare coffee as needed

    Serve customers in a friendly manner

    Fill out a variety of paperwork

3. _____

    Knowledge of cash register functions

    High school degree preferred

    Ability to communicate effectively in English

    Knowledge of arithmetic and some bookkeeping

    Ability to work under pressure

4. _____

One week after final selection

5. _____

In the Personnel Office

JOB ANNOUNCEMENT 3

1. _____

DIETARY CLERK

2. _____

One year of hospital and food service experience

Ability to read and understand oral and written instructions in English

Knowledge of types of diets preferred

Ability to use computers

3. _____

Receive and process written diet orders for all patients

Handle communications by computer and phone

Maintain diet office files

Write and update patient menus

Check trayline to assure accuracy of patient trays

4. _____

Needed immediately

5. _____

Talk to Dietary Clerk Supervisor.

Look at the three job announcements again.

1. Do any of the jobs require previous experience? Which ones?

2. Find the job announcement that mentions education requirements. What does it say?

3. Which job announcements say that it is necessary to have good writing skills? What do they say?

LISTENING FOR DETAILS

Watch all the episodes again with the sound on. Listen carefully. Episodes 4 and 5 both mention parts of a job announcement. Put a check mark when you hear a part of a job announcement. Share your answers with your classmates.

	EPISODE 4	**EPISODE 5**
job title		
job description, duties		
job qualifications		
starting date		
where to apply		

CONVERSATION PRACTICE

A. *Read the conversation between Maria and Phuong. They are discussing a job announcement. With your classmates find where they talk about each part of the job announcement.*

MARIA: Do you think I should apply for this job?

PHUONG: What position is it?

MARIA: Housekeeping Supervisor.

PHUONG: What is the job description? What are the duties of the job?

MARIA: It says here:

Responds well to individual guest's needs.

Communicates daily with staff and subordinates.

Attends regular departmental level meetings.

PHUONG: Would you like this job?

MARIA: Yes, I'd like this job very much.

PHUONG: Well, are you qualified? What are the requirements?

MARIA: These are the qualifications:

> *At least two years' experience as a housekeeper.*
>
> *Gets along well with a variety of people.*
>
> *And some experience as a supervisor is helpful.*

I have some experience as a supervisor.

I know how to make up a schedule.

I get along with people.

I think I am qualified.

PHUONG: I think you are too. You should apply.

B. *Work with a partner. Choose one of the three job announcements in* **Language Skills***. Student A asks questions about the following information:*

- job title, name of the job, position

- job description, duties of the job

- job qualifications

- starting date

- where to apply

Student B looks at the job announcement and answers the questions.

C. *With your partner write your own job announcement. Then ask and answer questions about it.*

Summary

Watch the Summary Presentation. Then read the summary below. Discuss any questions you have about Reading Job Announcements with your teacher and classmates.

When you know there's a new job, you have to read the job announcement. The job announcement tells you what you need to know about the job.

The job announcement:

- tells you the job title. The job title is the name of the job.
- gives you job qualifications. Job qualifications tell you what experience or training you need to get the job. Reading the job qualifications is very important before you apply for a job.
- gives you a job description. A job description tells you what you will do on the job. It may also be called "job duties."
- tells you the starting date. The starting date is the day you begin the new job.
- tells you where to apply. Be sure to check where you need to apply.

Cultural exchange

Discuss these questions. Share your answers with your classmates.

1. Are job announcements used in your country? When? In what kinds of companies? What kinds of jobs are listed?

2. What information is in a job announcement?

3. If job announcements are not common in your country, how do people find out about job information?

4. Why are job announcements important in the United States?

5. Will reading a job announcement help you in a job interview in the United States? Why?

CONTACT ASSIGNMENT

A. Go to Personnel or Human Resources at your company or school and get two job announcements. For each one list the following information:

	JOB ANNOUNCEMENT 1	JOB ANNOUNCEMENT 2
Job Title	_____	_____
Job Qualifications	_____	_____
	_____	_____
	_____	_____
	_____	_____
Job Description	_____	_____
	_____	_____
	_____	_____
	_____	_____
Starting Date	_____	_____
Where to Apply	_____	_____
Hourly Wage	_____	_____

B. Work with a partner. One partner is the interviewer; the other is the employee. Practice doing a job interview.

Small Talk

LEARNING TO LISTEN

Thinking about the Topic

This lesson is about small talk.

STUDENT

CONVERSATION 1

First watch Student Conversation 1. Then answer the questions. Share your answers with your classmates.

    1. What is small talk?

    2. When should you make small talk?

    3. Why is small talk important?

First Impressions

EPISODE 1

Watch Episode 1 with the sound off. Think about these questions.

    1. Where does the scene take place?

    2. Who are the three people?

    3. What are they talking about?

    4. How do they feel about one another?

Brainstorm

Share your answers to the questions above with your classmates. Tell how you know the answers.

60

Main Idea

Watch Episode 1 again <u>with the sound on</u>. What is the main idea? Use these questions to help you find the main idea.

1. What are the three people talking about?

2. What is the problem?

3. What does the younger woman do to help solve the problem?

Work in a small group. Try to agree on the best answers. What new information did you get with the sound on?

Predict

What do you think Episode 2 will be about? Why? Share your thoughts with your classmates.

First Impressions

Watch Episode 2 <u>with the sound off</u>. Think about these questions.

1. Where does the scene take place?

2. Who are the two people?

3. What are they talking about?

4. How do they feel about each other?

Brainstorm

Share your answers to the questions above with your classmates. Tell how you know the answers.

Main Idea

Watch Episode 2 again with the sound on. What is the main idea? Use these questions to help you find the main idea.

1. What are the two people talking about?

2. What is the problem?

3. What is the solution to the problem?

Work in a small group. Try to agree on the best answers. What new information did you get with the sound on?

STUDENT

CONVERSATION 2

Watch Student Conversation 2 with the sound on. What do you think Episode 3 will be about? Share your thoughts with your classmates.

Main Idea

Watch Episode 3 with the sound on. What is the main idea? Use these questions to help you find the main idea.

1. What has changed?

2. Who solved the problem? How did he solve the problem?

3. How does Mrs. Madison feel now?

Work in a small group. Try to agree on the best answers.

STUDENT

CONVERSATION 3

Watch Student Conversation 3 with the sound on. Discuss these questions. Share your answers with your classmates.

1. Why was Boju afraid to make small talk?

2. Does Boju now think it is difficult to make small talk?

3. How many examples of small talk can you find? What are they?

4. What are other examples of small talk?

CHECK YOUR UNDERSTANDING

A. *Read the conversation from Student Conversation 1. Then answer the questions.*

BOJU: Julio, do you know what "small talk" is?

JULIO: Yes. That's like friendly conversation. Like saying "Hello" or talking about the weather. Asking "How are you?"

BOJU: Yeah. Like asking about someone's health or telling them they have nice clothes on.

1. Julio and Boju say that small talk is friendly conversation. It's like saying "Hello" and:

   a. talking about _____

   b. asking _____

   c. telling someone _____

2. What are some other things people talk about when they make small talk?

3. What do you usually talk about when you make small talk?

B. *Read the information in the box.*

> GOOD SMALL TALK
>
> When someone makes small talk with you, you should:
>
> • Answer the speaker (you can agree or disagree).
>
> • It is important also to give new information *or* ask a question that keeps the conversation going.
>
>   A: What do you think of that camera?
>   B: It works very well. I really like the flash.
>   A: I really like chocolate ice cream do you?
>   B: Yes, but I prefer strawberry. Do you like that too?

C. *Circle the best answer.*

EXAMPLE   I can't believe how good you look in red.

    a. Oh yeah, I know.

    (b.) Thanks. My mother made this for me.

    c. Thanks.

---

1. I can't believe how cold it is today. Can you?

    a. Well, I don't think it's really cold.

    b. No, I've got to go.

    c. No, I can't either. Do you think tomorrow will be cold?

2. Did you see my new earrings?

    a. No. They're lovely. Where did you get them?

    b. No, I didn't see them. I'm really busy now.

    c. Yes, I did. Did you pick up the mail?

3. I'm glad we had a chance to talk.

    a. Yes, me too.

    b. Me too. I really enjoyed talking to you.

    c. Yeah, but I'm late now.

4. How was your weekend?

    a. It was OK, I guess. Not great.

    b. OK, I guess.

    c. Not great. How was yours?

5. That team really played a good game, didn't they?

    a. Yes, they did. Did you see that home run?

    b. I don't know.

    c. I guess so. I have to go.

D. *Decide if each answer below is **good small talk** or **poor small talk**. If it is good small talk, check whether the response **asks a question** or **adds a comment**. If it is poor small talk, check that box. Remember to check only ONE box.*

	GOOD SMALL TALK		POOR SMALL TALK
	ASKS A QUESTION	ADDS A COMMENT	NO QUESTION NO COMMENT

EXAMPLE **Person A:** What a great game!
Person B: Yeah. Did you see that goal?

ASKS A QUESTION	ADDS A COMMENT	NO QUESTION NO COMMENT
✓		

	GOOD SMALL TALK		POOR SMALL TALK
	ASKS A QUESTION	ADDS A COMMENT	NO QUESTION NO COMMENT

1. **A:** How are you?
   B: I'm fine. How are you?

2. **A:** How are you?
   B: OK

3. **A:** Do you like your new class?
   B: Yeah.

4. **A:** What a pretty blouse!
   B: Thanks. I made it myself.

5. **A:** Can you feel the heat today?
   B: Yes.

6. **A:** What did you do this weekend?
   B: Nothing.

7. **A:** I'm so pleased you stopped by.
   B: Me too. It was great to see you.

8. **A:** Thank you for inviting me to dinner.
   B: Thank you. I had a good time too.

9. **A:** I really enjoyed the piano player.
   B: Yes, it was a great concert. I love that kind of music.

10. **A:** Do you really like that soup?
    B: No.

LANGUAGE SKILLS

Read the following situations and complete the conversations. Be sure that your response:

- answers the speaker

- gives new information *or* asks a question that keeps the conversation going

EXAMPLE

Boju is Mrs. Madison's attendant in the retirement home. Mrs. Madison hurt her back, and she is still in bed today.

Mrs. Madison: Oh, Boju. How are you?

Boju: Fine, Mrs. Madison. How is your back today?

1. Aakhu and Maria are students at Wilson School. They're studying English.

Maria: Aakhu, your haircut looks great.

Aakhu: _____

2. Ms. Clemens is Boju's supervisor. She thinks he's a good worker.

Ms. Clemens: Boju, you have been doing excellent work.

Boju: _____

3. Julio comes to work on Monday morning and sees Jim, his supervisor.

Jim: How was your weekend, Julio?

Julio: _____

4. Julio and Boju and their teacher are talking in the hall.

Teacher: Hi, Julio. How did you like that book?

Julio: _____

LISTENING FOR DETAILS

Watch all the episodes with the sound on. Answer these questions. Share your answers with your classmates.

Episode 1

    1. Does Boju answer Mrs. Madison's questions?

    2. Does Boju make a comment or ask another question?

    3. Does Ms. Clemens answer Mrs. Madison's questions?

    4. Does Ms. Clemens make a comment or ask another question?

Episode 3

    1. Does Boju answer Mrs. Madison's questions?

    2. Does Boju make a comment or ask another question?

CONVERSATION PRACTICE

Work with a partner. Practice making and responding to small talk. Student A begins the conversation below. Student B responds by (1) agreeing or disagreeing; (2) asking a question or adding a comment. Then switch roles.

1. Student A: What a lovely day!

    Student B: _____

2. Student A: Did you see my new _____?

    Student B: _____

3. Student A: _____ was a very good movie, wasn't it?

    Student B: _____

4. Student A: Wasn't that a great game of softball (or soccer, or football) last night?

    Student B: _____

5. Student A: That was a hard assignment, wasn't it?

    Student B: _____

6. Student A: I think it's going to snow.

    Student B: _____

7. Student A: I really like Woody Allen. Do you?

    Student B: _____

8. Student A: Wow! that was a wonderful party, wasn't it?

    Student B: _____

9. Student A: *Jeopardy* is a great game.

    Student B: _____

CULTURAL EXCHANGE

Discuss these questions. Share your answers with your classmates.

1. Do you have "small talk" in your language?

2. What are three topics you make small talk about in your language?

a. _____

b. _____

c. _____

3. Give an example of how you make small talk with someone in your country.

SUMMARY

Watch the Summary Presentation. Then read the summary below. Discuss any questions you have about Small Talk with your teacher and classmates.

Small talk is *very* important. Small talk can be about many things.

Small talk is:

- talking about how someone feels
- talking about the weather
- giving and receiving compliments
- offering assistance
- talking about sports

CONTACT ASSIGNMENT

A. Listen to a conversation at work or at school between native speakers of English. Answer the questions. Then share your answers with your classmates.

1. How did the first speaker begin the conversation?

_____

_____

2. What did the first speaker talk about?

health

weather

sports

clothes

something else

3. What new information did the second speaker add?

_____

_____

4. What question, if any, did the second speaker ask?

_____

_____

B. Work with a partner. Tell your partner about a time when someone began to make small talk with you. Did you respond? What did you say?

Reading Work Forms

LEARNING TO LISTEN

Thinking about the Topic

This lesson is about how to read work forms.

First watch Episode 1. Then answer these questions. Share your answers with your classmates.

    1. How do Aakhu and Julio feel? Why?

    2. What forms do you use at work?

    3. What information do forms ask for?

    4. Is it difficult to fill out forms? Why or why not?

    5. How do you feel when you need to fill out forms?

Main Idea

Watch Episode 2 <u>with the sound on</u>. What is the main idea? Use these questions to help you find the main idea.

    1. Who are the people in this scene?

    2. What are they talking about?

    3. What is the problem?

    4. How do you know?

Work in a small group. Try to agree on the best answers.

Summary

Watch the Summary Presentation. Then read the summary below. Discuss any questions you have about Reading Work Forms with your teacher and classmates.

When filling out forms at work, you just need to look for some common words on each form, like:

- form name
- name
- date
- time
- location

They may be in different places on the form, so you have to look for them.

Check your understanding

Circle the correct answer.

EXAMPLE   Which one is the name of a form?

   a. Completed by Boju

   b. Repair Request

   c. Time started

1. Which one asks for your name?

   a. Date started

   b. Accident Report

   c. Completed by

2. Which one asks for the time?

    a. Room number

    b. Total time

    c. Maintenance Report

3. Which one asks for the location of your work?

    a. Date of injury

    b. Time started

    c. Building

4. Which one asks for the date?

    a. Floor

    b. Time In _____ Time Out _____

    c. Date completed

5. Where do we usually find the name of the form?

    a. in the middle of the form

    b. at the top of the form

    c. on the back of the form

6. Julio fell and hurt his leg. Which form does he need to fill out?

    a. Repair Request form

    b. Work Order form

    c. Work Injury form

7. Aakhu needs to write down when she arrives and when she leaves. Which form should she use?

    a. Time Sheet

    b. Apartment Maintenance form

    c. Service Request form

LANGUAGE SKILLS

A. *Read what Phuong says from Episode 2.*

PHUONG: Yes. You might not understand every word on the forms. They aren't so scary. Just look for places to put information like the date, your name, the time, and a location.

Put the information in boldface next to the right word or words.

EXAMPLE   Susan fell down and hurt her foot on **May 6, 1993**.

date started _____

date _____

date completed _____

date of injury _____ May 6, 1993 _____

1. Aakhu works at **Store 55**.

    building number _____

    address _____

    store number _____

2. Phuong arrived at work at **6:00 A.M.** and left **at 3 P.M.**

    time occupied _____ time vacated _____

    time in _____ time out _____

    time of day _____ A.M. _____ P.M.

3. Boju cleaned **the area around the tennis courts.**

address _____

location _____

building _____

unit _____

4. Maria broke a glass and cut her finger **at 2:00 in the afternoon.**

time spent _____

time vacated _____

time of accident _____

time in _____

5. Julio cleaned seven rooms and then filled out a daily cleaning report.

approved by _____

work done by _____

building number _____

location _____

6. Maria began cleaning Floor 22 on **December 7, 1992.**

time vacated _____

date of accident _____

date of injury _____

date started _____

7. Julio finished fixing the sink on **January 3, 1993.**

employee name _____

building number _____

date begun _____

date completed _____

B. *Look at the forms. Put the correct number next to the part of the form.*

1. name of the form   **4.** location

2. your name   **5.** time

3. date

EXAMPLE

HOUSEKEEPER: 2		DATE: 3	
	ROOM REPORT	LINEN COUNT	TIME 5
ROOM # 4			

HOUSEKEEPER'S REPORT 1

FORM 1

S E R V I C E   R E Q U E S T

Date _____   Time Spent _____

Location _____

Completed by _____

Remarks _____

FORM 2

MAINTENANCE REQUEST

TIME _____   DATE _____

BY _____   FLOOR _____

HOURS WORKED _____   BUILDING _____

DESCRIPTION _____

_____

_____

FORM 3

Work Accident

_____
(employee name)

_____   _____
(place of accident)   (date and time of injury)

_____   _____
(description of injury)   (place where injury occurred)

C. *Read the conversation.*

AAKHU: So, I'll be OK if I look for those words on the form.

JULIO: Exactly.

AAKHU: And I have to read the forms carefully to find these words.

JULIO: Yes, you can do it!

Circle the correct answers. Share your answers with your classmates.

1. About how many *common* words do you find on work forms?

    a. 20–30

    b. 100

    c. 5–6

2. Which three kinds of information do employers often ask for on work order forms?

    a. car license number

    b. location

    c. date started

    d. driver's license

    e. date completed

3. Which three kinds of information do employers often ask for on accident forms?

    a. your name

    b. your bank account number

    c. location

    d. time

    e. name of your teacher

4. Which three kinds of information do employers often ask for on daily cleaning reports?

       a. room number

       b. guest's name

       c. today's date

       d. your birthday

       e. completed by

5. Which three kinds of information do employers often ask for on repair requests?

       a. apartment number

       b. time of accident

       c. completed by

       d. building number

       e. date of injury

6. Which three kinds of information do employers often ask for on apartment maintenance forms?

       a. completed service on _____
                               (date)

       b. time of accident

       c. store number

       d. work done by

       e. apartment number

D. *Work with a partner. Use the information in the boxes to fill out the forms. Talk about any differences in where to put the information.*

1.

HOUSEKEEPER: DATE:

	ROOM REPORT	LINEN COUNT	TIME
ROOM #			

HOUSEKEEPER'S REPORT

Phuong Vann arrived at the hotel at 9:00 A.M. She cleaned Room 205 from 9:15 A.M. to 9:35 A.M. She changed two sheets and two pillowcases. She cleaned Room 207 from 9:50 A.M. to 10:15 A.M. She changed four sheets and four pillowcases. She cleaned Room 209 from 10:20 A.M. to 10:40 A.M. She changed one sheet and one pillowcase.

2.

S E R V I C E   R E Q U E S T

Date _____   Time Spent _____

Location _____

Completed by _____

Remarks _____

Julio Garcia received a request to repair the sink in an apartment. He went to Apartment 5 in Building 3. He repaired the sink on May 3, 1994. It took thirty minutes to repair the sink. He noticed a broken blind and repaired that too.

3.

MAINTENANCE REQUEST

TIME _____   DATE _____

BY _____   FLOOR _____

HOURS WORKED _____   BUILDING _____

DESCRIPTION _____

_____

The rug in the entrance hall in the main building needed special vacuuming. The hotel is very proud of the entrance hall on the main floor of its hotel. It is a very big room. Boju Khotari went there at 7:00 P.M. and worked until 8:30 P.M. to finish the job.

4.

Work Accident

_____
(employee name)

_____   _____
(place of accident)   (date and time of injury)

_____   _____
(description of injury)   (place where injury occurred)

Aakhu Brown fell and broke her arm on Sunday evening. It was a compound fracture. She was working in the store when she fell near the Coke machine. Someone had spilled Coke on the floor. It was close to closing time, around eleven o'clock at night. Too bad. It was July 7, her birthday.

LISTENING FOR DETAILS

Watch Episode 2 again with the sound on. What are the parts of a form?

_____

_____

_____

_____

_____

CULTURAL EXCHANGE

Discuss these questions. Share your answers with your classmates.

1. Is it usual to fill out forms at jobs in your country?

2. What kinds of forms do you fill out?

3. What information do they ask for?

CONTACT ASSIGNMENT

A. What are the names of the forms you use at work? (If you are not working now, ask a friend or a family member to get some forms for you.)

_____

_____

_____

B. Look at some of the forms and write the words they use to ask:

Your name   _____

_____

Location of your work   _____

_____

_____

Date   _____

_____

Time   _____

_____

C. Interview two people you know who are working now. Ask:

- What forms do you use at work?

- Are they difficult to fill out?

- How often do you need to fill out forms?

- What information does each form ask for?

Share the information with your classmates. Compare the types of forms you found out about. How many types are there?

UNIT 7
Asking for Clarification

• •

LEARNING TO LISTEN

Thinking about the Topic

This lesson is about asking for help when you don't understand.

STUDENT

CONVERSATION 1

First watch Student Conversation 1. Then answer these questions. Share your answers with your classmates.

1. What can you do when you don't understand someone?

2. What can you say when you don't understand?

3. Why is it important to say something when you don't understand, especially at work?

First Impressions

Watch Episode 1 with the sound off. Think about these questions.

1. Where are the two women?

2. What is their relationship?

3. What are they talking about?

Brainstorm

Share your answers to the questions above with your classmates. Tell how you know the answers.

Confirm

Watch Episode 1 again with the sound on. Work in a small group. Review your answers to the questions above. Try to agree on the best answers. Did your answers change? What new information helped you find the best answers?

First Impressions

Watch Episode 2 with the sound off. Think about these questions.

1. Where are the two women?

2. Who are they?

3. What are they talking about?

4. How do you think the younger woman feels?

Brainstorm

Share your answers to the questions above with your classmates. Tell how you know the answers.

Main Idea

Watch Episode 2 again with the sound on. What is the main idea? Use these questions to help you find the main idea.

1. What is the problem?

2. Who created the problem?

3. How did they solve the problem for the patient?

Work in a small group. Try to agree on the best answers. What new information did you get with the sound on?

STUDENT

CONVERSATION 2

Watch Student Conversation 2 with the sound on. Discuss these questions. Share your answers with your classmates.

1. What does Maria say it is important to do?

2. What did Maria do when she didn't understand?

3. Tell about one time when you asked for help when you didn't understand.

4. Tell about one time when you didn't ask for help when you didn't understand.

Action Plan

Do you want to watch Episode 3 <u>with the sound on or off</u>? Decide with your classmates. Talk about reasons why it is helpful to have the sound on. Then talk about reasons why it is helpful to have the sound off. Make a decision.

Main Idea

Watch Episode 3 <u>with the sound on or off</u>. What is the main idea? Use these questions to help you find the main idea.

> **1.** Where are the two women?
>
> **2.** What is the problem?
>
> **3.** What solution did they find?

Work in a small group. Try to agree on the best answers.

STUDENT

CONVERSATION 3

Watch Student Conversation 3 <u>with the sound on</u>. Discuss these questions. Share your answers with your classmates.

> **1.** Phuong says if you don't ask, there can be problems. What are they?
>
> **2.** Maria says if you don't ask, there can be problems. What are they?
>
> **3.** What will Phuong do next time?

CHECK YOUR UNDERSTANDING

A. *Read the conversation. Then answer the questions.*

JUDY: There is some broken glass. I need someone to clean up.

MARIA: The glass is not clean? You need a clean glass?

JUDY: No. No. There is broken glass on the floor of the bathroom. I need someone to clean it up!

MARIA: Excuse me. Please speak more slowly.

JUDY: I'll show you. There is broken glass. I need someone to clean it up.

MARIA: Ah, yes. I understand. You want me to clean up the glass from the floor.

1. Does Maria want to help Judy?

2. What does she do when she doesn't understand what Judy wants?

3. What questions does Maria ask to help her understand?

   a. _____

   b. _____

4. Maria still doesn't understand Judy. What does Maria say?

5. What do you say when you don't understand?

WHAT is asking for clarification? When you don't understand, you can ask for clarification. You tell the speaker which word or words you don't understand. You ask the speaker to make a word or a phrase clear.

B. *Read the conversation and circle the ways Phuong asks for clarification.*

MS. ADAMS: Phuong, you made a serious mistake tonight. You must change the IV bottle before it's empty.

PHUONG: I am sorry. I don't understand. I change the bottle when it's empty, right?

MS. ADAMS: No, *before*! *Before* it's empty!

PHUONG: I'm sorry. I still don't understand. Can you say it another way?

MS. ADAMS: Change the bottle with some solution in it—not when it is empty.

PHUONG: Oh. I understand now. I must change the bottle with some solution in it, not when it is completely gone.

MS. ADAMS: That's right. Now go check Mrs. Asato's solution.

C. *Here are some ways to ask for clarification. Write the way Phuong asks for clarification.*

1. Tells the speaker she didn't understand

_____

2. Asks for repetition

_____

3. Asks the speaker to say it another way

_____

4. Repeats the sentence and asks for confirmation

_____

5. Repeats the word she didn't understand

_____

6. Repeats to be sure she understood

_____

D. *Read Student Conversation 3. Then answer the questions.*

MARIA: It's difficult for us, but in this country when you don't understand, you have to ask. Don't be afraid to ask!

PHUONG: Yes. If you don't ask, it can be dangerous. I could have hurt the patient. I could have lost my job!

MARIA: When you don't ask, people get angry. They think you don't want to help them. They think you are wasting their time.

PHUONG: Next time I don't understand, I'll ask for help.

1. It is important to ask for help. What are the three reasons Phuong gives?

a. _____

b. _____

c. _____

What are the three reasons Maria gives?

a. _____

b. _____

c. _____

2. Can you think of other reasons why it is important to ask for help when you don't understand?

a. _____

b. _____

c. _____

WHY is it important to be very clear about instructions?

- So you can do your job well.

- So you don't get into dangerous situations.

- So you don't make mistakes. If you make a lot of mistakes, supervisors or customers can get angry at you.

E. *Circle **true** or **false** for each statement below.*

EXAMPLE	It's important to ask for clarification so you don't make mistakes.	(TRUE)	FALSE

1. If you don't understand something, it is better to keep quiet and wait to ask a co-worker later. TRUE FALSE

2. Ask for clarification when you don't understand all or part of what someone says to you. TRUE FALSE

3. Asking for clarification means that you understand what the person said but you want more information than you already have. TRUE FALSE

4. You may need to ask more than one question when you want clarification. True False

5. To clarify something means to make it clear. TRUE FALSE

LANGUAGE SKILLS

A. *Read the information.*

When you ask for clarification, follow three basic steps:

1. Identify the information you need.

2. Decide *why* you didn't understand it.

- Was it the meaning of a word or a phrase?

- Did the speaker speak too fast?

- Did the speaker speak too softly?

3. Ask for clarification. When you ask, say clearly what your problem is.

WAYS TO ASK FOR CLARIFICATION

There are several ways to ask for clarification. Always be as specific as possible.

When you don't understand anything, you can say

- I'm sorry, I don't understand.

- Please repeat.

- Please speak more slowly.

When you *still* don't understand, you can say:

- I'm sorry. I still don't understand. Can you say it another way?

If you don't understand one word, for example, the word *before*, you can say:

- What does *before* mean?

- *Before*?

- You want me to do it *before*?

It is good to repeat what you heard to make sure you understand.

- OK, I need to pick up milk, bread, and onions.

B. *Circle the best answer.*

EXAMPLE

"I want you to fix the *air conditioner* right away." You don't understand the word *air conditioner*. You can say,

    a. "Could you speak more slowly, please?"

    (b.) "You want to me fix the . . . ?"

    c. "Right away?"

1. "Check the *thermometer* to be sure that the temperature is correct." You don't understand the word *thermometer*. You can say,

    a. "I don't understand."

    b. "What does *thermometer* mean?"

    c. "Check the temperature?"

2. The hotel guest is speaking to Maria. The guest is very upset about the broken glass. She is speaking very quickly. Maria doesn't understand much. What can Maria say?

    a. "What does that mean?"

    b. "What?"

    c. "I don't understand. Could you say that more slowly?"

3. Ms. Adams says, "You must change the IV bottle *before* it's empty." Phuong doesn't understand Ms. Adams. What can Phuong say?

    a. "I'm sorry. I don't understand."

    b. "Can you please speak more slowly?"

    c. "I still don't understand. Can you say it another way?"

4. Maria's supervisor says, "Maria, I need you to put the shampoo, conditioner, deodorant, soap, and shower caps into all the baskets." Maria is thinking: "This is a big job. What a long list! I'd better check to be sure I remember everything." Maria can say,

    a. "Put shampoo, conditioner, deodorant, soap, and shower caps in all the baskets?"

    b. "Could you tell me that again? I don't understand."

    c. "What does *deodorant* mean?"

5. Julio's supervisor asks, "Julio, did you *splice* those two wires together yet?" Julio doesn't understand *splice*. What can he say?

    a. "Um, I'm not sure."

    b. "I'm sorry. I understand wires but I don't understand the other word, *spli . . .*? What does it mean?"

    c. "Please slow down. I don't understand you."

6. Boju's supervisor says, "Boju, you have to check the *odometer* to be sure that the mileage is correct." Boju doesn't understand *odometer*. What should he say?

    a. "I don't understand."

    b. "What does *odometer* mean?"

    c. "Check the mileage?"

7. Ms. Adams is talking to Phuong. Phuong doesn't understand many of the words. What can Phuong say?

    a. "What does that mean?"

    b. "What?"

    c. "I don't understand. Could you say that more slowly?"

Work with a partner. Discuss why you chose your answer. Find the best answer. Share your answers with the whole class.

C. *Read the situations and complete the dialogues. Ask a clarifying question or ask about the underlined words.*

EXAMPLE

Boju is Mrs. Madison's attendant in the retirement home. Mrs. Madison is waiting for her daughter to come visit her today.

Mrs. Madison: Oh, Boju. How are you?

Boju: Fine, Mrs. Madison.

Mrs. Madison: Boju, <u>would you mind</u> taking a look out the window to see if my daughter has arrived yet?

Boju: *I'm sorry, Mrs. Madison. What does "would you mind" mean?*

Mrs. Madison: That's just a polite way of asking if it is OK with you to do something.

Boju: Sure, I'd be glad to check the window.

1. Maria and Julio are playing billiards. Maria is thinking about her next play. There's a lot of noise in the room. Maria didn't hear Julio very well.

Julio: Maria, have you seen the new movie . . . yet?

Maria: _____

2. Ms. Clemens is Boju's supervisor. She wants him to do a safety check.

Ms. Clemens: Boju, I want you to pull all the <u>fire extinguishers, fire hoses, and fire axes</u> and check to make sure that they are working properly.

Boju: _____

Ms. Clemens: Yes, that's right. Check all three.

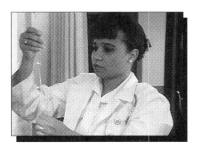

3. Phuong is a nursing assistant in the hospital. Ms. Adams is teaching Phuong how to set up intravenous monitors on the patients.

Ms. Adams: OK. First you thread the line through here. Do you see?

Phuong: Yes, ma'am.

Ms. Adams: Next you clamp it here. Check the reading on the monitor. If it is 75 or above, no problem. But if it is below 75, you have to take everything out and check for a <u>bend in the hose</u>.

Phuong: _____

Ms. Adams: Oh, that just means that you will make sure that the hose is not turned or twisted and cutting off the movement of liquid.

4. Julio is being trained to use a new wet vacuum. His supervisor has just shown him how to start it. The vacuum is running and it's very noisy. Julio didn't understand a word.

Julio: _____

Supervisor: The supervisor turns off the vacuum and talks to Julio. You're right. I couldn't hear you either. Now, let's go over it again.

5. Maria has applied for health care at her job. She has to see the personnel counselor to answer some questions.

Counselor: How many <u>dependents</u> do you have?

Maria: _____

LISTENING FOR DETAILS

Watch all the episodes again <u>with the sound on</u>. Answer these questions.

1. Count the number of times Phuong and Maria ask for clarification. Write the number here. Compare your results with your classmates.

   Episode 1 _____

   Episode 2 _____

   Episode 3 _____

2. Give one or two examples of the ways Phuong and Maria ask for clarification.

3. What did Phuong do when she didn't understand in Episode 1? What happened when she didn't ask for clarification?

CONVERSATION PRACTICE

Choose a topic from this list:

The Best Meal I Ever Had

My Favorite Television Program

My Most Important Decision

My Favorite Relative

The Most Beautiful Place in My Country

Work in pairs. Student A talks on the topic for one or two minutes. Student B asks for clarification at least three times. Take turns. Write down the questions you asked. Then share your questions with your classmates.

SUMMARY

Watch the Summary Presentation. Then read the summary below. Discuss any questions you have about Asking for Clarification with your teacher and classmates.

When you don't understand, you should say:

- I'm sorry. I don't understand.
- Can you say it another way?
- Please speak more slowly.

When you don't understand a word (for example, *before*), ask, "What does *before* mean?" or say the word you don't understand: *"Before?"*

CULTURAL EXCHANGE

Discuss these questions. Share your answers with your classmates.

1. How do you look when you don't understand?

2. What do you do with your head, eyes, and hands when you don't understand?

3. What do you say in your country when you don't understand someone at work?

CONTACT ASSIGNMENT

A. Listen to native English speakers at work or at school. List three ways you hear them ask for more help when they don't understand.

1. _____

2. _____

3. _____

B. The next time your teacher gives you an assignment, ask for clarification. Compare your requests with your classmates. Discuss if asking for clarification helped.

Responding to Instructions

LEARNING TO LISTEN

Thinking about the Topic

This lesson is about how to respond to instructions.

STUDENT CONVERSATION 1

First watch Student Conversation 1. Then answer these questions. Share your answers with your classmates.

1. Your boss asks you to do something. What should you do?

2. Your boss asks you to do something. You don't know how to do it. What should you do?

3. Your boss asks you to stay late. You have a doctor's appointment. What should you do?

First Impressions

Watch Episode 1 with the sound off. Think about these questions.

1. Where are the two men?

2. What are they doing?

3. What is their relationship?

4. What are they talking about?

Brainstorm

Share your answers to the questions above with your classmates. Tell how you know the answers.

Main Idea

Watch Episode 1 again with the sound on. What is the main idea? Use these questions to help you find the main idea.

1. What is the problem?

2. What is the reason for the problem?

3. How does this episode end?

Work in a small group. Try to agree on the best answers. What new information did you get with the sound on?

STUDENT

CONVERSATION 2

Watch Student Conversation 2 with the sound on. Discuss these questions. Share your answers with your classmates.

1. Julio and Maria are talking about responding to instructions. Why didn't Julio follow his supervisor's instructions?

2. Maria didn't follow her supervisor's instructions. Are Julio's and Maria's reasons the same?

3. What are two reasons for not following instructions?

4. Can you always respond to instructions in school or at work? Why or why not? Tell about one time when you didn't respond to instructions. What happened?

First Impressions

EPISODE 2

Watch Episode 2 with the sound off. Think about these questions.

1. Where are the three women?

2. What are they doing?

3. What is their relationship?

4. What are they talking about?

Brainstorm

Share your answers to the questions above with your classmates. Tell how you know the answers.

Main Idea

Watch Episode 2 again with the sound on. What is the main idea? Use these questions to help you find the main idea.

1. What does Maria tell her co-worker?

2. What does Maria tell her supervisor?

3. What is the problem?

Work in a small group. Try to agree on the best answers. What new information did you get with the sound on?

First Impressions

Watch Episode 3 with the sound off. Think about these questions.

1. Where are the two women?

2. What is their relationship?

3. How do they feel about each other?

4. What are they talking about?

Main Idea

Watch Episode 3 again with the sound on. What is the main idea? Use these questions to help you find the main idea.

1. What problem do the two women discuss?

2. Do they solve the problem?

Work in a small group. Try to agree on the best answers. What new information did you get with the sound on?

Main Idea

Watch Episode 4 with the sound on. What is the main idea? Use these questions to help you find the main idea.

1. What does Maria's co-worker ask her?

2. What does Maria answer?

3. How does the episode end?

Work in a small group. Try to agree on the best answers.

Predict

What do you think Episode 5 will be about? Why? Share your thoughts with your classmates.

Action Plan

Do you want to watch Episode 5 with the sound on or off? Decide with your classmates. Talk about reasons why it is helpful to have the sound on. Then talk about reasons why it is helpful to have the sound off. Make a decision.

Main Idea

Watch Episode 5 with the sound on or off. What is the main idea? Use these questions to help you find the main idea.

1. Who are the people?

2. What is their relationship?

3. What are they talking about?

4. How does the episode end?

Work in a small group. Try to agree on the best answers.

Main Idea

Watch Episode 6 with the sound on. What is the main idea? Use these questions to help you find the main idea.

1. What are Maria and her supervisor talking about?

2. Why is the supervisor angry?

3. How does the episode end?

Work in a small group. Try to agree on the best answers.

STUDENT

CONVERSATION 3

Watch Student Conversation 3 with the sound on. Discuss these questions. Share your answers with your classmates.

1. What can happen if you do not respond to instructions?

2. What can you do if you cannot follow instructions?

3. What suggestions do Julio and Maria make?

4. What other suggestions can you think of?

CHECK YOUR UNDERSTANDING

A. *Read the information.*

> It's important to repeat your supervisor's instructions to be sure that you have heard and understood all the information and what you need to do first. If you do not understand what you need to do on the job, you can:
>
> • make mistakes
> • cause an accident
> • make your supervisor angry

B. *Read the instructions Julio's supervisor gives him. Then answer the questions.*

BOB: Now the main thing to remember is to never mix these two together. Together they are dangerous.

(Julio doesn't say anything. He picks up the two cleaners and goes to clean the bathroom.)

1. Did Julio repeat his supervisor's instructions to make sure that he understood them?

2. Did Julio look at the labels on the cleaners before he began to clean?

3. Why did Bob, the supervisor, warn Julio?

4. Have you ever had problems when you didn't repeat instructions back to the supervisor? What happened?

5. Have you ever had problems because you didn't read the label on a product? What happened?

C. *Circle the response that repeats all the instructions.*

EXAMPLE   **Supervisor:** Unpack those boxes in the corner and stack them over here.

     a. Do you want me to do something else after that?

     (b.) Unpack these boxes and put them here in this corner, right?

     c. Unpack those boxes?

1. **Supervisor:** Check the 5th and 8th floors for dirty linen and bring it to the laundry.

     a. Take it to the laundry and then check the other floors, right?

     b. Check the 5th and 8th floors right now, right?

     c. Check the 5th and 8th floors, and take the dirty linen to the laundry, right?

2. **Supervisor:** First take an inventory of the snacks, and then restock the shelves up front.

     a. Take the inventory of the snacks at the front of the store, right?

     b. Do an inventory of the snacks and the restock the front shelves, right?

     c. Restock and then take inventory, right?

3. **Supervisor:** Check on Mrs. Madison and see if she wants to take a walk or play cards in the meeting room.

     a. Ask Mrs. Madison if she'd like to play cards or take a walk, right?

     b. Check on Mrs. Madison and take her to play cards, right?

     c. Ask Mrs. Madison what she would like to do this afternoon, right?

4. **Supervisor:** Be sure to take some soap to Room 619 and then go to the laundry to pick up some towels.

     a. Go to the laundry and then take soap to Room 619, right?

     b. Take some soap to Room 719, right?

     c. Take some soap to Room 619 and then pick up towels, right?

LANGUAGE SKILLS

It's important to repeat instructions to be sure that you understand them correctly. Read the instructions below. Work with a partner and think of appropriate responses. Write the responses and then practice giving instructions and responding. Take turns.

1. **Supervisor:** Be sure to mix one cup of flour with two cups of water.

   _____

2. **Supervisor:** Be sure to put the linen into the laundry basket and take the glasses to the kitchen.

   _____

3. **Supervisor:** I also want you to clean rooms 323, 345, 376, and 380.

   _____

4. **Supervisor:** Please be sure to check on Mrs. Smith and Ms. Jones before you start to work with Bob.

   _____

5. **Supervisor:** Never mix these chemicals together. Together they are dangerous.

   _____

LISTENING FOR DETAILS

Watch all the episodes again with the sound on. Answer these questions. Share your answers with your classmates.

Episode 1

1. Did Julio ask his supervisor for more information about his work?

2. Did Julio read the labels before using the cleaners?

Episode 2

1. Did Maria explain her problem to her supervisor?

2. What reason did Maria give for not doing what her supervisor asked?

Episode 3

1. What reason did Alicia give for not doing what her supervisor asked?

Episode 4

1. What problems did Maria cause?

2. Why didn't Maria tell her supervisor she could not work?

3. Alicia and Maria both had good reasons. Why did the supervisor get angry at Maria but not at Alicia?

CONVERSATION PRACTICE

It is important to tell your supervisor why you may not be able to do something. If you don't, you can cause problems, and your supervisor may get angry. Read the conversation between Ms. Campbell and Maria.

MS. CAMPBELL: Why didn't you tell me that yesterday? You caused a lot of problems when you left without telling me. The manager was very angry. The guests were unhappy. And some other housekeepers had to stay late to finish your work.

MARIA: I was afraid. I was afraid to tell you that I couldn't stay late.

MS. CAMPBELL: It's better to tell me if you can't finish the job. It can cause a lot of problems if you don't. In the future, be sure to tell me.

What three problems did Maria cause? Write your answers here. Then share them with your classmates.

1. _____

2. _____

3. _____

Now work with a partner. Read the situations below. Make up conversations between a supervisor and a worker. Practice the conversations and then switch roles.

1. Situation: The worker cannot finish waxing the floor because he or she feels sick. The worker must speak to the supervisor.

2. Situation: The worker cannot attend the morning meeting because he or she has a doctor's appointment. The worker must speak to the supervisor.

3. Situation: The worker is unable to clean a bathroom on the second floor because a maintenance person is working on the sink. He or she must explain the situation to the supervisor.

4. Situation: The worker is unable to clean the meeting room because meetings have been scheduled all day. He or she must tell the supervisor.

5. Situation: The worker cannot stay late to do some extra work because his or her child is sick. The worker must tell the supervisor.

Summary

Watch the Summary Presentation. Then read the summary below. Discuss any questions you have about Responding to Instructions with your teacher and classmates.

Responding to instructions is very important.

If you want to get the job done right:

- Check your understanding with the boss. When the boss gives you instructions, you should repeat the instructions to make sure you understand.
- Read the instructions on the label. Labels are important because they tell you what to do, and they tell you what not to do.

When you can't do what the boss wants, be sure to:

- say you can't
- say why you can't

Cultural exchange

Discuss these questions. Share your answers with your classmates.

1. In your country what do people do when they don't understand instructions? What do they say?

2. In your country what do people do when they can't do what their boss asks them to do? What do they say?

CONTACT ASSIGNMENT

A. Practice repeating instructions to your supervisor (or your teacher if you are not working now). Does it help you understand better? When you did not understand, did your supervisor (or teacher) help you understand? How?

_____

_____

_____

_____

_____

B. Read the labels on the three different chemicals or materials you use at work or at home. List the words you do not understand. Look up the words in a dictionary or ask a co-worker, your supervisor, or your teacher the meanings of these words. Write the words and the meanings here.

_____

_____

_____

_____

_____

C. Ask a co-worker or a friend about a time when he or she was unable to complete a supervisor's instructions. Ask _why_ he or she didn't complete the instructions and what was said to the supervisor. Tell the story to the class. You can write notes here to remember it.

_____

_____

_____

_____

_____

UNIT 9 — Asking to Change Your Work Schedule

LEARNING TO LISTEN

Thinking about the Topic

This lesson is about changing your work schedule.

STUDENT CONVERSATION 1

First watch Student Conversation 1. Then answer these questions. Share your answers with your classmates.

1. How do you change your work schedule?

2. When do you ask to change your work schedule?

3. Is it difficult for your boss to change your schedule? Why or why not?

First Impressions

EPISODE 1

Watch Episode 1 with the sound off. Think about these questions.

1. Where are the two men?

2. What are they doing?

3. What is their relationship?

4. What are they talking about?

Brainstorm

Share your answers to the questions above with your classmates. Tell how you know the answers.

Main Idea

Watch Episode 1 again with the sound on. What is the main idea? Use these questions to help you find the main idea.

1. What are the two men talking about?

2. Does Julio get what he is asking for?

3. How does Julio ask his question?

4. What reason does Mr. Walters give for his answer?

Work in a small group. Try to agree on the best answers. What new information did you get with the sound on?

STUDENT

CONVERSATION 2

Watch Student Conversation 2 with the sound on. Discuss these questions. Share your answers with your classmates.

1. Mr. Walters doesn't change Julio's work schedule. Does Julio think that Mr. Walters was fair? How do you know?

2. Do you think that Mr. Walters should change Julio's schedule? Why or why not?

3. What are some good reasons to ask for a change in your work schedule?

Main Idea

EPISODE 2

Watch Episode 2 with the sound on. What is the main idea? Use these questions to help you find the main idea.

1. Where are the man and the woman?

2. What is their relationship?

3. What are they talking about?

4. What is the result of this conversation? How do you know?

Work in a small group. Try to agree on the best answers.

Predict

What do you think Episode 3 will be about? Why? Share your thoughts with your classmates.

Action Plan 1

Do you want to watch Episode 3 with the sound on or off? Decide with your classmates. Talk about reasons why it is helpful to have the sound on. Then talk about reasons why it is helpful to have the sound off. Make a decision.

Action Plan 2

If you decide to watch Episode 3 with the sound on, make a list of the words you expect to hear.

If you decide to watch Episode 3 with the sound off, make a list of the new information you want to watch for.

Main Idea

Watch Episode 3 with the sound on or off. What is the main idea? Use these questions to help you find the main idea.

1. Who are the people?

2. What is the problem?

3. How do they solve the problem?

Work in a small group. Try to agree on the best answers.

STUDENT

CONVERSATION 3

Watch Student Conversation 3 with the sound on. Discuss these questions. Share your answers with your classmates.

1. What questions does Julio ask Aakhu?

2. What does Aakhu answer? What three suggestions does she give to ask for a change in her work schedule?

3. What reason did Julio give for not getting a change in his schedule? Does Aakhu think that Julio had a good reason?

4. Did you ever ask for a change in your work schedule? What happened? What reason did you give?

CHECK YOUR UNDERSTANDING

A. *Read the conversation between Julio and Mr. Walters. Then circle the correct answer.*

JULIO: Mr. Walters! I need to talk to you. You have to change my work schedule to the day shift!

MR. WALTERS: That's very interesting. I *have* to change your schedule. And is there a good reason for this— demand?

JULIO: Well, I have a new girlfriend! Right now we're on opposite shifts, so there's no time to see her.

EXAMPLE   A work schedule is:

     a. the days and hours you work.

     b. a list of the jobs you have to do each day.

     c. asking for more information.

1. Julio wants to change his schedule because:

     a. He wants to go to school.

     b. He wants to see his girlfriend.

     c. He wants to help the company.

2. The best way to begin to ask for a schedule change is to say:

     a. You have to change my schedule right away.

     b. I must change my schedule right now.

     c. May I talk to you about my schedule?

3. Mr. Walters is angry because:

  a. Julio demands a change.

  b. Julio has a girlfriend.

  c. Julio is late for work.

4. Julio's reason for changing his schedule is:

  a. a good reason.

  b. not a good reason.

  c. an important reason.

5. Mr. Walters will probably:

  a. say yes because Julio is a good employee.

  b. say no because he doesn't like Julio.

  c. say no because Julio doesn't have a good reason.

B. *Read the information. Then circle the correct answer.*

There are three things to do to change your work schedule.

1. State your needs.

    Maria: Mr. Garcia, may I speak to you for a moment? If it is possible, I really need to change my schedule to the evening shift.

2. Give a good reason

    Maria: My children are going to be home in the morning, and I need to take care of them.

3. Negotiate the change

    Mr. Garcia: Well, Maria, I understand your problem. But I need some time to re-do the schedule so that everything is covered. Can you wait for two weeks?

    Maria: Of course, I can wait for two weeks. The children get out of school in three weeks. Would that be long enough for you to make the change?

    REMEMBER: Give your supervisor as much time as possible to make the change. Always talk to your employer at a good time. Don't ask him or her when it is very busy and there is not enough time to think.

1. A good way to begin your request for a schedule change is:

    a. Excuse me, Mr. Walters. May I talk to you about my schedule?

    b. Excuse me, Mr. Walters. I must change my schedule.

    c. Excuse me, Mr. Walters. I need a new schedule or I quit.

2. A good reason to ask for a schedule change is:

    a. transportation problems.

    b. cold weather.

    c. a visit from your brother.

3. Based on the example of Maria and Mr. Garcia, *Negotiate the change* means that:

  a. Maria makes the decision to change her own schedule.

  b. Mr. Garcia makes the decision to change Maria's schedule.

  c. Mr. Garcia and Maria discuss her schedule and decide together.

4. When you negotiate a change in schedule, you should:

  a. demand a change right away because you need it.

  b. understand that it takes time to change schedules.

  c. switch with a worker without telling your supervisor.

5. If you want to change your schedule, you should:

  a. know in advance which shifts you can work.

  b. ask for an immediate schedule change.

  c. quit if you don't get what you want.

6. You should ask your supervisor for a schedule change:

  a. first thing in the morning when he or she is busy.

  b. at the end of the day when he or she is ready to go home.

  c. by asking what is a good time to see him or her.

7. You should ask your supervisor for a schedule change:

  a. three days before you need it.

  b. as soon as possible before you need it.

  c. one day before you need it.

8. You need to understand:

  a. The supervisor must change your schedule if you ask.

  b. The supervisor may not be able to change your schedule.

  c. The supervisor probably won't change your schedule.

LANGUAGE SKILLS

Work in a small group. Read the following situations, and discuss how to ask for a change in schedule. Try to agree on the best way, and write it in the spaces. Share your thoughts with your classmates.

1. Julio is going to college at night, but he doesn't want anyone to know in case he doesn't do well. He just got his class schedule for next week. He talks to Mr. Walters, his supervisor, at 8:00 A.M. when he gets into the office about changing the days Julio works. How should Julio ask for a change?

    a. State your needs.

Julio: _____

_____

    b. Give a reason.

Julio: _____

_____

    c. Negotiate the change.

Mr. Walters: I can't do that right away. Can you wait a few days?

Julio: _____

_____

2. Dung's car isn't working, and she needs to come to work by bus. She is afraid to travel at night. She wants to work the day shift. How should Dung ask for a change in her work schedule?

    a. State your needs.

Dung:_____

_____

    b. Give a reason.

Dung:_____

_____

c. Negotiate the change.

Mr. Wong: I can work out the change. I need some more time, though. Can you wait until the end of the month?

Dung: _____

_____

3. Maria's sister is returning to Argentina and can't take care of her children anymore. Maria can work only the night shift. That way her husband can take care of the children.

a. State your needs.

Maria: _____

_____

b. Give a reason.

Maria: _____

_____

c. Negotiate the change.

Ms. Clemens: I will speak to the other housekeepers. Can you work the day shift some of the time?

Maria: _____

_____

LISTENING FOR DETAILS

Watch all the episodes again <u>with the sound on</u>. Answer these questions. Share your answers with your classmates.

Episode 1

    1. Why does Julio want to change his schedule?

    2. When does Julio want to change his schedule?

    3. Why does Mr. Walters say it's difficult to change Julio's schedule?

Episode 3

    1. Why does Aakhu want to change her schedule?

    2. When does Aakhu want to change her schedule?

    3. When can Steve change her schedule?

    4. What will Aakhu do until Steve can change her schedule?

CONVERSATION PRACTICE

Work with a partner. Practice asking to change your work schedule. Take turns as the boss and as the employee. Decide what your job is. Then think of two situations when the employee needs to change his or her work schedule. Role-play the conversation.

EXAMPLE   Situation: José's daughter begins school this year. José must take her to school. He needs to arrive fifteen minutes later each day. Then he will leave fifteen minutes later. José generally opens the store, so it will be difficult for his boss.

José: Ms. Smith, I would like to change my schedule.

Ms. Smith: Why?

José: I must take my daughter to school each day. Then I will arrive fifteen minutes later at 8:15. I won't be able to open the store. But I could stay fifteen minutes later. Is that possible?

Ms. Smith: I can't change your schedule this week but I can next week. Can you find someone to take your daughter to school this week?

José: Yes, my sister can help me this week. Thank you very much.

When you are the employee, remember to:

- state your reason for the change
- give a good reason
- be prepared to negotiate

When you are the boss, be sure to:

- ask for a reason for the change
- give a reason why you cannot do exactly what the employee wants (can't do it right away, can't give all the days asked for, can't give the shift asked for but can give another)

Summary

Watch the Summary Presentation. Then read the summary below. Discuss any questions you have about Asking to Change Your Work Schedule with your teacher and classmates.

> To change your work schedule, do three things:
>
> - state your needs
> - give a good reason
> - be willing to negotiate

Cultural exchange

Read what Aakhu says about changing a work schedule.

AAKHU: It's not easy to change someone's schedule. When you want to change your shift, you should ask in advance so he has enough time to make the change.

Discuss these questions. Share your answers with your classmates.

1. What reasons do people in your culture give for a schedule change?

2. When do people in your culture ask for a schedule change or a few days off? What do they say?

3. When do American employers expect you to ask for a change? What may happen if you do not give the employer time to make the change?

CONTACT ASSIGNMENT

A. Think of three reasons why you might need to ask for a change in your work schedule.

1. _____

2. _____

3. _____

B. Interview an employer you know. Ask him or her what was the best reason an employee gave to change a work schedule. Ask what was the worst reason. Ask what was the funniest reason.

_____

_____

_____

_____

_____

C. Ask a friend about a time he or she had to change a work schedule. Ask why he or she had to change the schedule, what was said, and what the employer said. Was he or she successful? Then tell the story to the class. You can write notes here.

_____

_____

_____

_____

_____

_____

UNIT 10 Safety on the Job

LEARNING TO LISTEN

Thinking about the Topic

This lesson is about safety.

STUDENT
CONVERSATION 1

First watch Student Conversation 1. Then answer these questions. Share your answers with your classmates.

    1. When should you give a safety warning?

    2. What are some safety words?

First Impressions

EPISODE 1

Watch Episode 1 with the sound off. Think about these questions.

    1. Where are the two men?

    2. Who are they?

    3. What are they doing?

    4. How do they feel about each other?

Brainstorm

Share your answers to the questions above with your classmates. Tell how you know the answers.

Confirm

Watch Episode 1 again with the sound on. Work in a small group. Review your answers to the questions above. Try to agree on the best answers. Did your answers change? What new information helped you find the best answers?

First Impressions

Watch Episode 2 <u>with the sound off</u>. Think about these questions.

1. Where are the two men?

2. Who are they?

3. What happens?

4. How do they feel about each other?

Brainstorm

Share your answers to the questions above with your classmates. Tell how you know the answers.

Main Idea

Watch Episode 2 again <u>with the sound on</u>. What is the main idea? Use these questions to help you find the main idea.

1. What are the two men talking about?

2. What is the problem?

Work in a small group. Try to agree on the best answers. What new information did you get with the sound on?

First Impressions

Watch Episode 3 <u>with the sound off</u>. Think about these questions.

1. Where does the scene take place?

2. Who are the three people?

3. What is their relationship?

4. What happens?

5. How do the two women feel about the man?

Brainstorm

Share your answers to the questions above with your classmates. Tell how you know the answers.

Main Idea

Watch Episode 3 again with the sound on. What is the main idea? Use these questions to help you find the main idea.

    1. What are the three people talking about?

    2. What is the problem?

Work in a small group. Try to agree on the best answers. What new information did you get with the sound on?

STUDENT
CONVERSATION 2

Watch Student Conversation 2 with the sound on. Discuss these questions. Share your answers with your classmates.

    1. Why is Julio annoyed and confused?

    2. How did he give each warning?

    3. Why didn't people listen?

    4. What does Maria suggest?

    5. How do you give safety warnings? What do you say?

Action Plan

Do you want to watch Episode 4 with the sound on or off? Decide with your classmates. Talk about reasons why it is helpful to have the sound on. Then talk about reasons why it is helpful to have the sound off. Make a decision.

Main Idea

EPISODE 4

Watch Episode 4 with the sound on or off. What is the main idea? Use these questions to help you find the main idea.

    1. Where are the man and the woman?

    2. What are they talking about?

    3. What is the problem?

    4. What is the solution?

Work in a small group. Try to agree on the best answers.

STUDENT

CONVERSATION 3

Watch Student Conversation 3 <u>with the sound on</u>. Discuss these questions. Share your answers with your classmates.

1. What happened to the people Julio warned?

2. Why did it happen?

3. What helps people listen to a warning?

4. What warning does Julio give Maria?

5. What is the best way to give a warning?

6. Did you ever give someone a warning? Did it stop an accident?

CHECK YOUR UNDERSTANDING

A. *Read the conversation from Student Conversation 3. Then answer the questions.*

JULIO: What a *bad* day! Nothing went right. I tried to warn people. I said, "Be careful," but they didn't listen and had accidents.

MARIA: You know, sometimes when you give a warning, you should also give a reason. You can tell the person what to pay attention to.

1. What happened to the people Julio talked about?

2. Did Julio try to help them? What did he do?

3. What else does Maria suggest Julio do to help them?

4. Why does Maria think this will help?

5. What are some other warnings like, "Be careful"?

B. *Read the following statements. Circle **True** if the statement is correct or true. Circle **False** if the statement is not correct or false.*

EXAMPLE	Giving a warning can help prevent accidents.	(TRUE)	FALSE

1. It's not necessary to give a warning because people already know about dangerous places at work.   TRUE   FALSE

2. If you give people a reason for your warning, they may pay more attention.   TRUE   FALSE

3. It's helpful to ask for a reason when you get a warning.   TRUE   FALSE

4. There are some special words that people usually use to give warnings.   TRUE   FALSE

5. Many labels have warning words.   TRUE   FALSE

6. It's not necessary to give a reason because people *never* pay attention to warnings.   TRUE   FALSE

7. Safety is the responsibility of every employee.   TRUE   FALSE

8. If you don't pay attention to safety words, you might get hurt.   TRUE   FALSE

C. *Look at each picture and read each dialogue. Circle the warning word. Then circle what to be careful of. Then underline the reason.*

EXAMPLE

JULIO:	(Watch out!)(Don't touch that pail.)
MR. MERCER:	Why?
JULIO:	It's dangerous. <u>It has chemicals in it</u>.
MR. MERCER:	Oh, OK. Let's move it carefully.

1. Julio: Look out!

    Janet: Look out for what?

    Julio: Look out for the cord. You might pull it out.

2. Maria: Be careful, Julio. Don't touch those pots.

    Julio: Why?

    Maria: They're hot.

    Julio: OK. I'll use a pot holder.

3. Maria: No! Julio! Julio! That's the food sink. It's only for washing food. Use the other sink.

    Julio: OK. Thank you. I forgot. It has been a bad day.

LANGUAGE SKILLS

A. *Read the following labels and signs. Circle the correct answer.*

EXAMPLE

These two chemicals are:

    a. not dangerous to put into the toilet.

    (b.) dangerous to put together.

    c. not used for cleaning.

1. This sign means:

    a. Walk faster when in this area.

    b. Slow down when walking in this area.

    c. Check for water on the floor in this area.

2. This sign means:

    a. The contents of the bottle should be heated carefully.

    b. The contents of the bottle will burn very easily.

    c. The contents of the bottle will evaporate easily.

3. This sign means:

    a. The area has high amounts of electricity that could hurt people.

    b. The area has high amounts of radioactivity that could hurt people.

    c. The area has high amounts of danger that could hurt people.

NO ENTRANCE

EMERGENCY EXIT ONLY

4. This sign means:

    a. You may enter but you may not exit through this door.

    b. You may exit in an emergency, but you may not enter.

    c. You may exit or enter in an emergency only.

**NO TRESPASSING
PRIVATE PROPERTY**

5. This sign means:

    a. You may drive in this area, but you must be careful.

    b. You may not drive in this area because the government owns the property.

    c. You may not drive in this area because the owners do not want you to.

B. *Work with a partner. Read the following situations. Then write in the reason.*

EXAMPLE   You want to warn a co-worker about a cord across the floor.

You say: Watch out!

There's a cord across the floor.

1. You are washing the floor when your co-worker starts to walk on the wet floor.

   You say: Look out!

   _____

2. The label on the bottle warns not to mix two liquids because they're dangerous.

   The label says: Don't mix these two liquids.

   _____

3. You are wearing gloves because there is a dangerous liquid in your pail. Your boss comes and begins to move the pail.

   You say: Don't move the pail!

   _____

4. A sign says This sink is only for washing food. Julio begins to put the dirty water from the floor in the sink.

   You say: Don't use that sink!

   _____

5. Julio is mopping the floor and walking backward. He is about to back into a cart full of wine glasses.

   You say: Be careful!

   _____

6. Maria goes to the kitchen to wash pots and pans. Maria is going to pick up a very hot pot to wash.

You say: Don't touch that pot!

_____

7. There is an open hole on the sidewalk. There is a sign to warn people.

The sign says: DANGER.

_____

8. Someone broke the glass in the cooler at the 7-Eleven. A repairman will come later to replace the glass. There is a sign to warn people.

The sign says: BE CAREFUL!

_____

9. No one should use the elevator when there is a fire. There is a sign on the hotel door to warn people.

The sign says: Don't use this elevator.

_____

10. Phuong didn't notice the emergency sign on the door at the retirement home. Aakhu tries to warn her.

Aakhu says: Be careful!

_____

LISTENING FOR DETAILS

Watch all the episodes again with the sound on. Answer these questions.

1. Count the number of times you hear a reason for the warning. Write the number here. Compare your results with your classmates.

      Episode 1 _____   **Episode 3** _____

      Episode 2 _____   **Episode 4** _____

2. Listen for one or two examples of warnings. Write them here. Share your examples with your classmates.

_____

_____

Summary

Watch the Summary Presentation. Then read the summary below. Discuss any questions you have about Safety on the Job with your teacher and classmates.

It's important to pay attention to warnings, and it's important to give warnings.

Sometimes it helps to give a warning and a reason. Then, people pay more attention to your warning.

When someone gives you a warning, you should ask for a reason:

- so you'll know what to do
- so you won't do it again

Cultural exchange

Discuss these questions. Then share your answers with your classmates.

1. Where do you see warning signs in your country? What do they say?

2. How do people in your country give warnings? What do they say?

3. Do they usually give a reason?

CONTACT ASSIGNMENT

Look around your workplace or your school.

1. Are there any signs that give warnings?

_____

2. Where are they?

_____

3. What warning words do they use? Write them here.

_____

_____

4. What reasons do the signs give for the warnings?

_____

_____

5. Did anyone give you a warning this week?

_____

6. What was the warning?

_____

7. What reason did she or he give for the warning?

_____

8. Did you listen to the warning? Why or why not?

_____

9. Tell your classmates about a time when you gave someone a warning. You can write notes here.

_____

_____

_____

_____